Germany and Scotland Immigrants in Iowa

Margaret Krug Palen

HERITAGE BOOKS
2019

HERITAGE BOOKS
AN IMPRINT OF HERITAGE BOOKS, INC.

Books, CDs, and more—Worldwide

For our listing of thousands of titles see our website at
www.HeritageBooks.com

Published 2019 by
HERITAGE BOOKS, INC.
Publishing Division
5810 Ruatan Street
Berwyn Heights, Md. 20740

Copyright © 2019 Margaret Krug Palen

Heritage Books by the author:
A Different World: My Life and Making a Difference in the World
Genealogical Guide to Tracing Ancestors in Germany
Genealogical Research Guide to Germany
German Settlers of Iowa: Their Descendants and European Ancestors
German Settlers of Iowa: Their Descendants and European Ancestors, Revised Edition
Germany and Scotland Immigrants in Iowa

All rights reserved. No part of this book may be reproduced or transmitted in any form or by any means, electronic or mechanical, including photocopying, recording or by any information storage and retrieval system without written permission from the author, except for the inclusion of brief quotations in a review.

International Standard Book Number
Paperbound: 978-0-7884-5902-3

Table of Contents

	Page
Preface	5

Part I
In farming is the strength of the people

Chapter 1 – Discovering the Past 9
Chapter 2 – Blending American Cultures 31
Chapter 3 – Life in Germany..43
Chapter 4 – Centuries of Farmers 51

Part II
While the earth remaineth, seedtime and harvest, and cold and heat, and summer and winter, and day and night shall not cease. Genesis 8:22

Chapter 5 - Twentieth Century USA.......................................57
Chapter 6 – Prairie Life 79
Chapter 7 – The Changing Seasons..99
Chapter 8 – The Tall Corn State..117

Part III
My heart will keep and ponder the things in this hour of grace

Chapter 9 – Extended Family Years 127

Part IV
One who does not toil for his country will give up oneself

Chapter 10 – Years of Change 145
Chapter 11 – Connecting With the Past 151

Part V
Endurance produces character; character produces hope...Romans 5:4

Chapter 12 Understanding Cultures 161

PREFACE

American immigrant ancestry has often been lost in the melting pot of our western nation. My interest in American culture and my academic pursuit of lifelong learning fostered a desire and ambition to search the writings of my ancestors and my forebearer's accounts of their lives and travel.

Theme headings dividing the parts of this book were discovered and translated from Gothic lettering painted on European village barns and homes of my ethnic European family heritage. They express the values of endurance, faith, and hope in the future.

My household was organized to begin the task of researching, reading writings from forbearers, and finding family records. Words became sentences, then paragraphs and chapters emerged. The ink stamps in my passports register every continent of the world and research in some countries many times. All in all, a great experience.

PART I

In farming is the strength of the people

CHAPTER 1
Discovering the Past

German and Scottish immigrants in Iowa were savers of history and genealogy and left many clues about their early life. Their view of the world and of their Old World European heritage relates to USA generations in the twentieth and twenty-first centuries.

An uncomplicated and uncompromising approach to life in Germany and Scotland gave emigrants little room for ambiguity throughout the Great Depression years of the twentieth century in America's Midwestern Iowa farm belt. Those years spanned a time of great change in the United States.

The story of all human progress is one of a struggle against all odds including warfare. From Abraham Lincoln we learned that our country was the last best hope of man on earth, built on heroism and noble sacrifice. When President Lincoln proclaimed the Homestead Act during the Civil War to disperse land west of the Mississippi River for settlement, because the population in the east was becoming too crowded and causing the war, the Krug ancestors left Bremen, Germany on the sailing ship *Columbus* and arrived in New York July 19, 1865 to establish their home in a land of liberty and freedom. They did not know Lincoln had been assassinated until they landed in New York. They rode a train from New York to cross the Mississippi River to the Louisiana Purchase land made available for homesteads at Cedar Rapids, Iowa. The train stopped along the way to pick up soldiers who were returning with the Iowa regiment from fighting in the Civil War. Uncle George Krug described what his father remembered of the appearance of the soldiers when they climbed directly onto the train all dirty, grimy and sweating from being in the Civil War battlefields.

Families that arrived from Germany continued their native language for two generations in America. The first generation born in America spoke only the English language and they were forbidden to learn the German language. All grandchildren were forbidden to speak the German language. Two wars with Germany in the twentieth century caused discrimination in The United States of America against people from Germany; therefore, speaking in the German language only existed among people who were from Germany.

German immigrants in America valued the virtures of faith, hope, and hard work. If they had wanted to bring the culture they fled with them, they would not have come in the first place; they would have stayed in their native land and tried to make the most of it there. The generations of German families that came to the New World came to become Americans and they constantly reminded the younger generation of that fact. They did everything within their power during their lifetime to develop their adopted country.

Before multiculturalism reared its head in America, in the latter part of the 20th century, it was not good to be an immigrant. Families changed their surnames to reflect a strong English trend of Americanism making it possible to be accepted with respect and without regard to emigration. The Krug family changed the pronunciation of their surname, a common word in the German vocabulary that meant "pitcher" a vessel with handle for pouring liquids, so that it sounded English and was not immediately identifiable with the country of its European origin. The 'r' in Krug was not rolled on the roof of the mouth as is the correct pronunciation in the German language; 'rug' was added to K giving it an English sound. Immigrant Great-Great-Grandfather Johann Justus Krug III was known only by the name Gus Krug in his USA lifetime.

The Bryner Scottish ancestors were listed in the first U.S. census taken in Pennsylvania after the American government was formed in 1776. It is not known what year the immigrant Bryner ancestors came to the New World in North America. A cousin, Minnie Bryner Bauer of Kewanee, Illinois, traveled to Bryner Ridge in Western Pennsylvania, near Ohiopyle, Fayette County, in June 1940 and found a descendant of the original Bryner family still living on the original Bryner homestead.

Great-Grandfather James Monroe Bryner married into the Gordon Highland clan of Scotland when he married Sarah Caroline Gordon and moved to Benton County, Iowa, in 1873.

The Gordon clan of Scotland traces its ancestry to Adam through each generation and the Kings of Scotland, descendants of Malcolm III. Great-Grandmother Sarah Caroline Gordon descended from James Gordon and was an immigrant to America in 1724. On January 1, 1900 Great-Grandmother Sarah Gordon's youngest child, Frank Arthur Bryner, married Inez Vivian Tanner, a descendant of the Scottish William Muirhead family of Glasgow, Scotland.

James Monroe Bryner and Sarah Caroline Gordon

Frank Arthur Bryner Sr. and Inez Vivian Tanner Bryner

The William Muirhead family of Glasgow became parents of twin sons in 1802. Twin George immigrated to America in 1849 and founded his family lineage; twin John immigrated to New Zealand as a missionary and it is where his descendants continue to live.

George Muirhead was a weaver by trade and made patterns for paisley shawls. He was in charge of weaving over many operators. He married Ann Benny, also of Glasgow, and had five children. Ann operated a confectionary and fruit store they owned in Glasgow while her mother looked after the children. Ann died of cholera soon after the birth of the last son John. Anne's mother died a week later of the same disease leaving George faced with the problem of caring for his five motherless children.

In 1849, George began to make plans to immigrate to the "New World" where speculators were describing in glorious words the opportunities to be had in America. George sold much of his property except for personal possessions such as books and furniture to take with him to his New World home. During this same time George courted a young lady, Mary

Morrison, twenty-three years of age. On August 14, 1849 they were married. Mary's parents were James and Jane Ann Morrison. Her father had been a weaver, later becoming a burger for the city of Glasgow. In connection with his job the Morrison children received free clothing and a free education from the city. Mary Morrison Muirhead had more education when she arrived in America than many women of her age.

In the late summer of 1849, George and his young wife, with his five children, set sail from Glasgow for Liverpool where they embarked on a small American sailing vessel, the *Thomas H. Perkins*, and began the long ocean voyage across the Atlantic to start a new life. Storms, seasickness, and the discomforts of ocean travel beset them. After some time at sea, John, not yet two years old, fell ill and died. To prevent the sharks from following the small vessel, the captain at once made plans for burial at sea. The grief-stricken family pleaded with him to let them keep the child until they reached land, and because he believed that they were not far from land, the captain finally yielded and agreed to defer the burial of the child as long as the boat was not harassed by sharks. Soon they sighted a little island off the coast of Newfoundland. The captain sent out a small boat with a few sailors, the mother and father, and the body of the tiny boy. In the sandy soil of the island the sailors dug a small grave and a short service was held. Returning to the vessel they arrived in Philadelphia in the fall of 1849.

The Muirhead family's original destination was Cumberland, Maryland where George's sister lived. When they arrived in Cumberland they found, unknown to them, that only a short time before his sister had returned to Scotland. Since their destination was unknown, and the cost of expressing personal property was great at that time, the family decided in Maryland to sell the books and pieces of furniture they had brought from Scotland.

Mary and George Muirhead

The sight of Dundee, Illinois on a map reminded them of Dundee, Scotland, and they concluded, with hope in their heart, that it must be settled by Scottish immigrants. They traveled on the Baltimore & Ohio Railroad to Pittsburg, Pennsylvania, where they took a boat down the Ohio River and into the Mississippi River, then through a canal to Chicago, which was then only a small town. There they sighted a burly Scotsman from Dundee, Illinois, and he took them in his rough wagon drawn by oxen to Kane County, Illinois, where they eventually purchased a farm and established a permanent home in Plato Township. A descendant of the original Muirhead family continues to live on that farm.

The second child of George and Mary Muirhead, Mary Janette, nicknamed "Nettie," attended Elgin Academy where she worked for her board and room. In the fall of 1868, at age sixteen, "Nettie" was sent by her parents to Newhall, Iowa, to help her older half-sister Ann, married to a Mr. Ellis. Ann's youngest child died and she was so overcome with grief that her father sent sixteen year old "Nettie" to help the stricken mother.

"Nettie" remained in Iowa, and after passing the teachers examinations, taught in the Doolittle School near the Ellis home. There she met Englishman William Allen Tanner, a school director. Their acquaintance turned into love and they were married on Christmas Eve 1869 when "Nettie" was seventeen years old and William was twenty-eight years of age.

"Nettie"

William Allen Tanner was township supervisor from 1869 to 1871. He was elected Justice of the Peace in 1874, reelected in 1876, and was a notary public. Originally he studied to be a lawyer, but returned to the farm to help his father. His mother descended from William and John Means, two generations of a family born in the 1600's in County Fermanagh, Ireland. She arrived in Boston, Massachusets October 1718.

Great-Grandfather William Allen Tanner's family arrived in Benton County, Iowa, from Ohio by prairie schooner train in 1857. The prairie schooner train was made up of lumbering covered wagons, loaded down with household goods, a plow lashed to the outside, hauled by six-horse teams and by three yoke of oxen, driven by sun-bonneted William women, while the men and older boys on horseback cracked their long, black, Allen snake whips and herded loose horses and cattle along the trail, deep in mud or dust. It took three weeks to cross the "black swamp" of Indiana on corduroy roads.

William Allen Tanner

Great-Great-Grandfather John Tanner was born in York, Pennsylvania, April 22, 1812 and was left fatherless along with five other children when he was a boy of four years. The first nine years of his life was spent in the state of his birth. His mother and stepfather then pushed out to find a home in the wilds of Ohio. John settled in Wayne County, which was at that time almost an unbroken forest, thinly settled where luxuries were unknown. In those days it took brave hearts and brawny arms to subdue the wilderness and make it blossom. Married and the father of four children, in 1856, John Tanner sought a further westward home for his family by crossing the Mississippi River at Sabula to Iowa on a ferry boat.

John Tanner

The John Tanner family first lived in Linn County, Iowa, with wife Isabel's brother, John Kearns, who had come earlier to the state. Later, the Tanner family settled twenty miles west of Cedar Rapids on land bought from the U.S. government for five dollars an acre. They were the first to "break" the land and built a temporary house of logs sawed into lumber at a local sawmill. Neighbors were few, the nearest Tanner thirteen miles distant.

Isabel Kearns Tanner

The only habitations in Iowa in 1857 were log cabins on the prairie, practically a wilderness of tall prairie grass, wild geese, pelicans and cranes. Buffalo had not long been extinct and their bones still lay on the prairie. Holes known as buffalo wallows were still visible.

John Tanner was one of nine men who organized the first election in Eldorado Township, Benton County, Iowa. John Tanner also established the first post office in Benton County, Iowa, known as William's Post Office. Mail was received by stagecoach. There were only three families living between them and the city of Cedar Rapids. People stopped to stay overnight with the Tanner family, who also cared for their animals, when they were traveling by wagon from Tama to Cedar Rapids. In a great snow storm one winter a man became lost on the road and froze to death between the Tanner residence and Cedar Rapids, Iowa.

A few years later, the Tanner family moved to a farm two and half miles south of Newhall in Benton County, Iowa. It was bare land and they planted all the trees, but one cottonwood that had been planted earlier by a previous owner of the land. The Tanner family planted a large orchard of plums, apples, Ben Davids, Duchess, wild crab, Transcendents, Tolman Sweet, Northern Spies, old-fashioned Snow apples, grapes, raspberries, and currants. The orchard, garden, barnyard and house-yard covered ten acres. The Tanners made a specialty of raising timber and fruit trees. At harvest time John Tanner traveled all over the area selling apples. He also had hives of bees which he cared for without wearing protection of any kind.

The white-painted, wooden Tanner house was six rooms besides pantry, porch and stairway. The barn was painted red. A chicken house was located out in the windbreak grove of trees north of the house. An old, one-room house was used as a shop and it had a garret where the Tanners kept their walnuts in winter. They raised cows to milk and sold cream to a man who came around the country and gathered it. The milk was fed to calves. They had only a few hogs.

Grandfather William Tanner and Grandmother "Nettie's" first child, Mary Isabel "Dolly" Tanner was born December 15, 1870 in the Tanner farm home where the young couple lived with his parents. "Nettie" became very ill after Dolly's birth. A woman attended at the birth and it was not a success. "Nettie" became delirious, and William procured a doctor. William never undressed for over a week, but just lay across the bed and rested when he could while attending to "Nettie's" recovery. Little "Dolly" became ill with cholera, died August 2, 1871, and was buried in the family plot in the Mound Cemetery at Watkins, Iowa.

Grandfather William Allen Tanner always wanted to see the mountains and after the death of little "Dolly" he decided, September 3, 1871, they should take a trip to Colorado. They were gone a little over a year and spent the time in Denver and

Georgetown. Grandfather William climbed Pikes Peak and made a cane out of a limb of a tree to use in climbing up and down the 14,110 foot mountain. He was sick afterward from the shock of his feet in the descent down the mountain. Meanwhile, Grandma "Nettie" worked part-time in a hotel until their return to Iowa, November 13, 1872. The rocks William collected were saved by "Nettie" all her life, and also by their daughter Inez who always treasured the mementos of her father.

Inez Vivian Tanner was born January 30, 1877 in the Tanner Benton County, Iowa, farm home. This time Grandma "Nettie" had a doctor and both mother and baby were healthy from the moment of birth. When Inez was a year old the parents and baby went to Illinois to visit the Muirhead relatives. While visiting Inez caught cold and got the croup and was very sick. Uncle George Muirhead called a doctor to attend to her. Thereafter, she was never sick with anything serious requiring a doctor.

September 1880, Grandma "Nettie's" sister Louella Muirhead came from Illinois to visit in the Tanner farm home. Grandpa William's brother Cicero Tanner was building a house as he was to be married. On Saturday, September 25, Grandpa William took a wagon to nearby Norway, Iowa, to put Louella on the train for her return to Illinois, and to pick up a load of lumber for the house his brother was building. It was raining and Mud Creek was overflowing its banks. About dusk, distressing cries were heard in the direction of Mud Creek, one and one-half miles north of Norway, which had the effect to instantly assemble an anxious throng with lanterns and rope. The crowd increased as it moved toward the creek hearing the cries which became more painfully audible that someone, they knew not who, was having a death struggle. Ropes were thrown in different directions without avail, when finally three determined young men plunged into the seething torrent and blackness of that swollen stream and rescued from the angry waters the almost lifeless body of Mr. Ellingson who had been in town with his team until nearly dark. Mr. Ellingson was at once taken to the nearest house where he died in the hands of his rescuers.

The next morning was Sunday and the lifeless team of horses of Grandpa William Allen Tanner of Eldorado Township was found imbedded in the murky stream. This at once congregated large groups to search for Grandpa William Tanner which unsuccessfully terminated with the darkness of night. The following Monday his body was found downstream clinging to a willow tree. It is thought that Grandpa William tried to cross the creek on a bridge just north of Norway so he could get home before it got dark instead of where the creek crossed the road nearer their home. The bridge weakened by the swirling flood waters, plunged the team and wagon into the swift current. The wagon was loaded with lumber and cement so the horses could not swim. Grandpa William was a good swimmer, but was caught by uprooted trees and swept downstream.

Grandma "Nettie" sent a telegram about his death to Illinois to her father, George Muirhead, and Louella Muirhead pasted it in her Bible where it remained permanently in possession of the family.

Grandpa William Tanner built the barn on his parent's farm in the summer of 1880, but did not get it quite finished before he was drowned. It was never finished. He had the contract for the farm after Great Grandpa John Tanner was through with it in consideration of Grandpa William's having built the barn, and his will stated Grandpa William's daughter was to inherit the farm upon his death. The Tanner parents had the right to live on the farm during their lifetime.

Grandma "Nettie" and daughter Inez made their home on the Tanner homestead for eleven years with in-laws John and Isabel Tanner following Grandpa William Allen Tanner's untimely death. The Benton County Court administered the property until Inez was legally of age to take control of her inheritance.

Inez Tanner Bryner remembered when she was growing up on the Tanner homestead, a short distance from U.S. Highway 30, how frightened she was when native American Indians came to their home to beg for food. Benton County was between the Tama County Sac & Fox Indian Reservation and the city of Cedar Rapids. The Indians were savage, warrior tribes that made noises on the kitchen porch when she was taking pie out of the oven and she immediately opened the door to find several hungry Indian warriors glaring at her. She remembered instantly handing them the pie because she was scared they would scalp her to get the food. She was forever puzzled about the timing of their arrival and thought they must have been able to smell the baking pie, but she preferred they have it rather than steal the chickens from the farmyard.

The first week of February 1891 Grandma "Nettie: and her daughter moved to Blairstown, Iowa, so Inez could be a high school student. It was the only high school in that part of the county at that time. October 7, 1891 Grandma "Nettie" was married in her Blairstown home to bachelor Bruner Lovaire Groff of Lancaster, Pennsylvania, who had driven cattle cross-country to Benton County, Iowa. Bruner Groff worked in Iowa for Lucious Doolittle husking corn during harvesting. Inez Tanner sewed his husking mittens and broke the sewing machine needle when it ran through her finger. Bruner Groff took her to the doctor and had the needle removed.

When Inez was seventeen years old she took the teachers examination and taught the spring and fall term in the Young School, two miles west of her home. Winter term she taught in her home school where she continued for four terms until she earned enough money to go to Tilford Academy in Vinton. There she met Frank Arthur Bryner, also a student at Tilford Academy and a teacher at a nearby Benton County school. They were married January 1, 1900.

Following the death of both Great Grandparents John and Isabel Tanner, and preceding the birth of a second child named Enid, Inez and Frank Bryner moved to the Tanner homestead, two and one-half miles south of Newhall, Iowa. They took possession, for the first time, of the land Inez inherited from her father at his untimely death when she was three years old. The birth of Enid was unexpectedly premature when she dropped out of her mother's womb onto the floor of their farmhouse on the Tanner homestead. Her mother Inez failed to consult a doctor during her pregnancy and developed phlebitis, called "milk leg" at that time. Dr. Bradley was called immediately from his office in rural Newhall to their farm home that was only a short distance away. Years later, Inez told how Dr. Bradley scolded her for not having consulted with him about her pregnancy before that time. Her explanation was that since she had already given birth two years earlier to a daughter named Hope she thought she knew everything about pregnancy, and therefore did not consult the doctor about her second pregnancy.

Grandma Mary Janette "Nettie" Muirhead Tanner Groff lived next door to Dr. Bradley in Newhall, Iowa, where Bruner Groff was a cattle buyer and operated a butcher shop, and she came immediately to care for the new premature baby. Since the baby's mother was too ill to care for the tiny infant, Grandma "Nettie" Groff took the baby to her home and placed it in a shoebox in the cookstove oven for warmth. Incubators were unknown in that day, but this method served as an incubator that successfully saved the premature infant life. Grandma "Nettie" remembered the loss of her daughter at a young age, and she was determined to save the life of her grandchild.

Enid continued to live in Newhall with her grandparents, Bruner Lovaire Groff and Mary Janette "Nettie," when more siblings were born. Her parents often moved and changed their way of making a living. The farm south of Newhall that Inez inherited when she was three years old, upon the 1880 death of her father William Allen Tanner, was sold and a newspaper which included a house was purchased in Wayne, Nebraska. While publisher and editor of *The Wayne Herald*,

Frank Bryner wrote on his newspaper letterhead to his parents dated September 22, 1906:

Dear Parents:

If you will think back about forty years you will remember of having moved out to Iowa and probably you did not write home as often as you ought, maybe you did not write at all.

I have a big undertaking on my hands and considerable to do and think about, as probably you did at my age, so you see how it is. I often think of you folks, the children talk about you so much, they are the right ages to talk and ask a great many questions. Hope was telling me, only a short time ago, that she had only one grandpa and two grandmas. When I told her I didn't have any she seemed to think it very strange. She has been advanced in school from the C class to the B class though she has gone only a little over two months, think there is a years work in each grade. At any rate the neighbor girl who started the same time Hope did is still in the C class. Hope got dissatisfied because they were all strangers in her new class and didn't want to go to school, so I went to the school house with her one noon and told the teacher I didn't want Hope to be in a class where she was not contented and would rather she would go back into the C class or I would keep her out of school as she was pretty young anyway.

The teacher begged me not to take her out of school, said she was the best one in her new class and it would be a shame to put her back in the

C class, said she would have a book in six weeks and be reading it. She didn't have such long hours when she was in the C class for they came home earlier. She seems contented now for the teacher lets her come home earlier than the rest of her class if she gets tired. I told her to for I don't believe in crowding her through just because she learns easily.

Enid doesn't grow much, she is very small by the side of Hope who is more than twice as large and looks after her like there might be five years difference in their ages.

We have moved from where we first lived when we came here, have a very nice house, small five room cottage with large garret for store room but it is neat and well built and is on the highest point of ground in the city with a large yard 150 ft. square. We are well pleased and think we have a model home. Our horse Bird is as fat as she can be, weighs 1,250 lbs. 300 lbs. more than she ever weighed before. We have a nice orchard and lots of fruit such as cherries, plums, apples, currents, gooseberries, etc.

Apples are cheap here the farmers can't sell them. I haven't tasted a watermelon this year, the cheapest one I have seen was 40 cents each and they are shipped in. They won't grow here. I have often thought I would like to be on the corner there where the melon wagons always are and buy one fresh from the patch for 10 cents. They are shipped from the western part of the state and ripen after they get here. Why didn't F. G. and Elvin come up to Wayne on their way out to Colorado?

Inez is real well but she never goes anywhere, doesn't go downtown more than once a month. She talks of going to the southeastern part of this state next week to visit a relative and get some peaches where they are 25 cents per bushel.

I can't come home now, I can't get away. I work from 6 o'clock in the morning to 9 o'clock at night, and my hired help cost me $41.00 per week.

Hoping to hear from you soon.

I am As Ever your son,

Frank

Enid Bryner in front of her parent's Wayne, Nebraska, home

The newspaper business was hard work and long hours. Frank Bryner sold his newspaper and Nebraska home and moved his family to Salina, Kansas in 1908. Enid visited her family every year at Christmas when her Grandma Groff took her by train to her family in Kansas. A postcard written October 29, 1909 by Inez to Enid after she traveled to Kansas and was returned to her grandparent's home again in Iowa reads as follows:

Dear Enid:

It was cold yesterday morning and Papa said he would like to see Enid come shivering out of her bedroom. I would like to see you too.

I expect you feel pretty fine with your new coat and hat. Have you plenty of hair ribbons? I will send you some if you need them. Tell me what color and how many yards.

With love, Mama

The Bryners owned a General Store and Frank was Postmaster in Kipp, Kansas 1909 to 1912. Grandpa Groff was Mayor of Newhall, Iowa, and owner of a meat market. He knew everyone in the rural town and about their business. One of the men in Newhall was going by train to visit relatives in Kansas in December, and he asked the man to escort Enid so she could visit her Kansas family and spent Christmas with them. She was seven years old when she wrote a postcard to her Grandpa Groff and he later returned it to her so that it became one of her precious possessions. She wrote the postcard Dec. 20, 1910 to Mr. B. L. Groff, Newhall, Iowa:

Dear Grandpa:

I have a good time.

From Enid

The Kansas wheat crops were failing and the wheat farmers came into the Bryner General Store to get groceries without any money. The Bryners let them charge the groceries until their accounts looked dangerously red. They sold out quickly and moved to Colorado where they went into business with a brother, five years older and unmarried. Together they bought and rented two houses in Cripple Creek, Colorado, the mining town with the famous "face on the barroom floor." They owned a tavern "pool hall" and cigar store in Canon City and lived in a home on the edge of the Royal Gorge. While there, Grandfather James Monroe Bryner came to join the family and climb by foot to the top of Pikes Peak, elevation 14,110 feet above sea level, a feat in that day. He died not long afterwards on December 02, 1911. The Bryner brothers sold out their Colorado property and moved again to Iowa. Frank and Inez Bryner bought another Iowa farm near Tileville in 1912, and purchased a farm in Dodge Township, Afton, Union County, Iowa, where their youngest child was born in 1914.

Inez Bryner sent a photo postcard to Enid dated November 8, 1912 postmarked Winterset, Iowa.

Dear Enid,

We are waiting to hear from you and Grandma. We have our out-side work most done now but it seems there are lots of little things to see to yet. Are you coming home this fall? Papa has one of our black pigs shut up and is feeding it all the corn it will eat. It is getting fat and will kill it as soon as it gets a little colder. We have had nice weather so far. Now write soon.

Love to all, Mama

When Enid finished eighth grade her grandparents sold their Newhall, Iowa, home and moved to Cedar Rapids, Iowa, so she could graduate from Washington High School that had an outstanding Iowa secondary curriculum. She enrolled in Coe College to earn a first-class teaching certificate and taught in rural, one-room, eight-grade schools for two years before marriage to a bilingual German-speaking grandson of immigrants from Germany.

CHAPTER 2
Blending American Cultures

The Cedar Rapids, Iowa, home of the Groff grandparents was the scene of a pretty wedding when their granddaughter was married. The wedding day dawned hot and dry in September. The temperature promised by the weatherman was predicted and was perfect for maturing the bumper corn crop rustling in the fields surrounding the eastern Iowa city.

The sun slanted brilliantly upon the large, buff colored frame and brick trimmed home on a high bluff of the Cedar River, on the northwest side of the city of Cedar Rapids, eighty miles west of the Mississippi River. The four bedroom house was surrounded by a large landscaped setting; a 500 foot front lawn of newly cut grass. There was a sun deck on the north side of a second floor bedroom and a full wall of windows in a bedroom on the south side of the house where the grandparents slept.

Preparation was in progress in the kitchen for serving a reception to sixty-five guests, just changed from fifty guests to accommodate the groom's Iowa relatives and the bride's relatives arriving at the front door of the Cedar Rapids home from Illinois.

A whirlwind-like flurry was going on to turn the parlor (a long, horizontal room from east to west — the entire front portion of the house, with open stairway at the west end) into a setting for a candlelight evening wedding. Home weddings were preferred society events, at that time, to church rites in the Midwestern Iowa city.

Cars parked for a short time under the extended entry porch roof where they could eventually drive forward and park in the backyard and exit down the 500 foot backside of the property to the country road and the city limits. Blue Jays in the surrounding giant native oak trees yelled without stopping "thief-thief" as they too became caught up in the excitement of the day.

In the kitchen a variety of fancy cakes and candied fruits were being arranged for serving. From the cellar of the large home came the thud, thud pounding of ice muffled by a wet gunny sack and the screech and groan of grinding ice and salt. Grandma "Nettie" Groff's brother, visiting from his farm in Illinois, was helping Grandpa Groff crank four freezers full of strawberry ice-cream made from home canned berries processed earlier in the summer.

The bride's mother rushed from one level of the home to another floor wiping her hands on her apron as she loped the three stories coordinating the activities in the big house. She and Grandma "Nettie" Groff made a good work team. Grandma "Nettie" Groff made all the decisions, but because of her advancing age and deteriorating health she did not do the physical work.

The bride's pretty ten year old sister, in her petticoat covered by a loose, wraparound robe, her hair in curlers, ran out to the clothesline in the backyard to help with the last of the laundry and shouted greetings happily to the bride as she passed the open doorway peeking at the wedding preparations.

The bride a tiny figure of barely five foot in height, erect posture and slightly built ninety-eight pounds, was named by her teacher educated parents after the character Enid in the tales of King Arthur. Her jet black hair softly curled around her head and her features were finely cut, her lips full; a square and serious face with eyes of dark piecing brown like her father's eyes. Though her expression was often melancholy there was a romantic appeal that permeated her appearance. After helping the women in the kitchen she hurried to the upstairs bedroom where she stacked into a neat pile the letters and valentines the groom had given to her over the past two years. Her deft fingers tied a neat satin ribbon around them, and formed the ends into a bow. Standing on her tiptoes she gently tossed the ribbon-bound, sentimental bundle onto the shelf of the bedroom closet, a place where they would lie undisturbed.

In the north bedroom with its adjoining roof deck, a display of presents for the bride and groom were carefully arranged. Gifts from a bridal shower a month earlier filled several tables: a quart jar of canned plums and a bread plate, gifts from two of the groom's aunts; a cookbook from farm neighbors of the Krug family; two aluminum pie pans from a friend of the bride; a glass pie pan from another neighbor of the Krug family; glass and aluminum mixing bowls; a sauce pan from the mother of the groom; a crocheted rug from the bride's mother; a sugar and creamer set from an aunt of the groom; four yards of toweling and a pair of pillow cases from first cousins of the groom; an embroidered Blue Bird design tablecloth from a school teacher friend of the bride; cake pans; a frying pan; flower sifter; funnel; strainer; bread baking pans; glass pickle dishes; doilies; and a variety of glass serving dishes from friends and neighbors of the bride and groom.

Wedding gifts accumulated as guests arrived for the ceremony. There were many practical gifts revealing divergent cultural values: a dish pan and dish cloth with $2 enclosed from the groom's paternal grandfather; a gold trimmed sugar and creamer set from two of the groom's bachelor uncles; six 1847 Rogers Bros. Ambassador pattern teaspoons to match the bride's choice of silverware given by a Krug aunt and uncle of the groom; six Community silverware teaspoons from a Groff neighbor; a dozen crackled design glass dessert plates from the wedding soloist and wedding pianis; a White sewing machine and handsewn silk quilt from the Groff grandparents; a large bowl Community silverplate serving spoon from an aunt of the groom; an eight day clock given by brothers and sisters of the groom; two milk setters from a Krug uncle and aunt of the groom; bread box; glass pie pans; three table cloths; Turkish towels; embroidered pillow cases; bed sheets; two embroidered luncheon cloths made by the bride's sister and a teacher friend; salt and pepper shakers; several pitchers of china and glass (Krug means "pitcher" in the German language); an aluminum double boiler; a Community silverplate butter knife and a jelly compote from Krug first cousins; a cut glass relish dish with three legs from Krug cousins; a bedspread from the grooms first cousins. Six plates, six cups and saucers in the Blue Bird pattern were given by an aunt and uncle of the groom; a copper tea kettle and an aluminum coffee pot given by four Happel aunts and uncles of the groom; another tea kettle and a roasting pan given by Krug first cousins; a glass pitcher given by the neighbors on the farm next to the groom's parents.

Envelopes and congratulation notes contained one and a half dollars and two one dollar bills. A Groff neighbor gave $5. The Illinois cousins of the bride gave a black and gold trimmed footed dish and matching saucer, and a crystal compote, and a bon-bon dish with metal holder, and six hand-painted dessert plates. Groff friends gave two hand-painted plates. The bride's mother gave a pair of glass candlesticks and a pink and white cotton quilt that she had made and quilted. The bride's brother gave a set of six kitchen cooking spoons and a pancake turner with holder. Six dining room chairs and a matching oak dining table were gifts of the bride's only aunt and uncle.

From morning until late into the afternoon Scottish relatives from Illinois worked feverishly with neighbor women carrying in bouquets of gladioli and white satin bows. The bride's cousin Althea Lewis of Elgin, Illinois, arranged them to form an altar on the far side of the parlor with floral bouquets, ribbons, and candles to make a romantic setting for the wedding.

A teenaged neighbor of the groom's family, also a school friend of the bride, was violin soloist at the wedding. She hurriedly climbed the stairway to the second floor when she arrived to converse with the bride. She remembered years later how she found the bride lying prostrate crosswise on the double bed in her Grandma Groff's bedroom crying. The tension of the day was too much for the fragile young bride.

The guests kept coming up the porch from the lawn where they waited in the warm summer air to converse before entering the large front room of the house. They listened to strains of music and settled comfortably into the rows of chairs facing the east wall with its floral banked altar. When the clock hands reached 8:00 p.m. the Rev. G. Rickels, pastor of St.Stephen's church, walked to the altar and motioned to the groom to start the ceremony. The bride's younger sister lighted the candles inserted in the floral greenery. Some of the guests turned their heads immediately to peer up the open stairway, but they could see nothing.

A neighbor sang, *Thanks Be to God* before the first strains of Mendelssohn's *Wedding March*. The bride's longtime school friend played the violin as the bridal party began desending the stairway.

The ring bearer was first cousin of the bride and the first to walk down the open staircase to the strains of Mendelssohn's *Lohengrin* music. She carried the rings for the double ring ceremony in two premier roses. The bride's Grandpa Groff gave her in marriage and helped her down the winding staircase. The bride leaned attractively on his arm, gowned in white silk crepe trimmed with lace and a veil of silk net formed a wreath with a tiara of orange blossoms. She wore white, buttoned, high heeled shoes and white silk hosiery. Her only jewelry was a string of pearls, a gift from the bridegroom. In her arm she carried a shower bouquet of sunburst roses. Her face was somber as she walked the narrow aisle from the west end of the room to the east wall bank of flowers, ferns and candlelight.

The tall, erect posture of Rev. Rickels quickly put everyone at ease as he lifted his eyes from his prayer book to look at the young couple. It was his custom to say a few words before the ceremony; a sermonette, about the value of home and family life. He concluded with thoughts about living a Christ centered life. A simple wedding ceremony followed, beginning with "Dearly Beloved. We are gathered here together in the sight of God to join this man and this woman in matrimony..."

When instructed to join hands, they exchanged rings. The groom gave the bride a script-engraved, white gold band: W.W.A.K. to E.M.B. 9-9-25. The bride slipped a simple gold 18 karat band on the groom's fourth finger, left hand. All heads bowed as the final prayer was delivered with the words, "whom God has joined together, let not man put asunder."

A neighbor was soloist and sang, *I Love You Truly*. It was a romantic moment in a candlelight setting. Everyone rose to their feet when the violin played a recessional and a line formed to shake hands with the newly married couple.

The wedding reception was served in the dining room. The bridal party was seated at the silver appointed dining room table centered with a pink and white wedding cake. The bride's Grandma Groff and her relatives from Illinois visited joyously, savoring the moment of reunion that brought them together.

The honeymoon did not begin until Scottish cousins Althea "Ther" and Elmer Lewis departed days later for Illinois and took the newly married couple with them to Chicago. "Ther" helped Great-Grandma Groff clean and put the house back in order again after the wedding and also devoted several days to visiting other Iowa relatives.

Mr. and Mrs. Walter W. A. Krug
September 9, 1925

The groom's parents held a Krug wedding reception at their home for all the relatives who could not be included in the wedding ceremony due to the small space in the Cedar Rapids home. The reception was held Thursday evening, September 13, at the Krug farm eight miles west of the city. One hundred and fifty aunts, uncles, and cousins attended. The groom had one-hundred first cousins descended from the ten brothers and sisters of his mother's family and the ten brothers and sisters of his father's family. The evening was filled with music and the playing of games. The color scheme was pink and white with zinnas, asters, foliage and flowers that decorated the farm house.

At the close of the extended family reception the young couple returned to Cedar Rapids to the Groff home where they joined the bride's Scottish cousins, Ther and Elmer, as passengers in the Lewis car to travel to Illinois.

Enid sent a picture postcard of the post office in Elgin, Illinois, to her Groff grandparents, that was postmarked September 15, 1925. The carefully saved sentimental postcard was later packed with Enid's wedding dress, veil, shoes and left-over engraved invitations:

Dear Grandparents:

We got to Elmers last night at 7:00 p.m. Had a lovely trip only for rain the last 90 miles. Walter drove for almost 80 miles and Elmer the rest. Althea didn't get to drive much. We are having a fine time. Haven't called on any of the other relations.

Love, Enid and Walt

A second postcard mailed four days later pictured Grant Park with the Field Museum and the new Stadium in Chicago:

Dear Folks:

Just got back from Chicago. Althea and Elmer took us in yesterday and we stayed all night and got back to Elgin about 6:30 p.m. Had a fine but tired time. Went through Marshall Fields Museum. Called on Uncle Will and Jim and Aunt Lou. Are invited to Will's and Jim's for a meal. Don't know when we'll be back.

Enid and Walt

The travel to Chicago was the farthest the groom had ever been away from his home. They were dined and entertained by Enid's Scottish family relatives; kind and gentle Protestant families of Glasgow stock. Enid's father's family was descended from the Scottish Highland Gordon clan. These strong divergent cultural strains met and married in America. The Groff grandparents were familiar with both the Scottish and German cultures and it was their wish that Enid marry Walter. They were sure she would be looked after and cared for the rest of her life, and Walter never forgot that he had discussed this with the Groff grandparents before their marriage.

In later years, Walter revealed that he never forgot that during their honeymoon Enid grabbed her purse and hit him over the head when he attempted to closely embrace her around her Illinois relatives.

The future for the newly married couple was a home on a farm owned by the Walter's parents in Benton County, ten miles west of the Cedar Rapids city limits. Their marriage brought together a strong cultural bond of family and religious values and their sixty year marriage spanned a time when farming was a successful family business.

Agricultural success in the United States of America launched generations into what was later called 'nuclear age families' from years of Iowa extended farming. Walter's father was Henry Krug of Löhlbach, Germany heritage who married Christina Marie Happel of Löhlbach, Germany heritage. They bought and managed four Iowa farms in an extended family farming system for their four married sons.

Wedding photo of Henry John Krug and
Christina Marie Happel, married March 9, 1898

Grandma Mary Janette "Nettie" Muirhead Tanner Groff, who raised Enid, had sterling silver braces placed on Enid's teeth to straighten them when she was young, and sent her to organ lessons, and then to Coe College to become a teacher. After Enid was married, Grandma Nettie gave her family money to have portraits made. The completed, mounted and framed photos then became the Groff's holiday and birthday gifts.

Both Enid and Walter used formal terms, *father* and *mother*, in speaking of their parents. Their language expressions were so respectful that they carried out the fourth commandment: "Thou shalt Honor thy father and thy mother that it may be well with thee, and thou mayest live long on the earth," and, Luther's explanation: "honor, serve and obey them and hold them in love and esteem." Some in the extended family continued to use what seemed like childish idioms in referring to parents and did not quit using those references.

CHAPTER 3
Life in Germany

Life in Germany at the time of immigration to North America was influenced by the 1284 AD Haina Kloster Monastery acquiring property in Sehlen from Count Gottfried von Ziegenhain, his wife and mother. A Count was an official to the Emperor and sent by either a Duke or an Emperor to negotiate or lead troops to protect borders. If the Count did well, for his merits he was given land and he also owned the people who lived on the land, and was responsible for their protection. Sometimes it was difficult for a monastery to maintain its property. There were protests from people and difficulties arising requiring treaties confirmed by the local court.

The Protestant Reformation in Germany as well as the abolishment of the Hessian monastaries by the Synod of Homberg in October 1526 did not bring much change to the land of my ancestors. Certainly the farmers hoped for liberation of their dependence on Haina Monastery, as the Abbot of Haina wrote in a letter that they already refused paying their tributes to the clergy, and the priests had to flee into the towns. This happened two years before Philip the Generous became a follower of Luther in 1524. My father's farming ancestors were disappointed. The property rights of the abolished monastery went over to the Prince of the country and he changed the monastery into a hospital using the income of the monastery for nursing inmates and to institute infirmed people. The monks of the Haina Monastery started the first Evangelical Lutheran church in Löhlbach at the time of the Reformation. Until that time Löhlbach villagers had no church.

Village of Löhlbach, Germany

With the abolishment of the monastery at Haina decisive changes in clerical activities came about. The four chapels in villages of the Bunstruth area of Hessen, where up to this time the four priest monks of Haina had held services, were torn down. The wood, bricks, doors, chalices and montrances were taken to Haina Monastery and the salaries of priests were reduced to the lowest possible amount. Great mischief and damage to the soul befell father's farming ancestors, and they prayed that a teacher of religion would be sent to them for their children.

The Prince introduced professional armies and expenses as a result and it compelled exact statistics as a base for taxation. In 1530, Sehlen records show twelve male persons fit for war, six unfit. This number nearly doubled until 1577. In the village register of the Grand Duchy of Hesse the community of Sehlen appears with twenty-six house owners, a number that has to be multiplied by five or six to get an idea of the number of inhabitants in those times.

The Thirty Years' War, 1618–1648, involved most of the countries of Western Europe and devastated much of Germany reducing the population by eleven million people. Private military entrepreneurs found opportunity during those years and the scale of their armies was great. Whole villages were burned and the land around them scorched.

The village of Löhlbach was burned and the church mined and destroyed by cannon fire in 1624-25. The altar cloth and communion ware was stolen. All church records were lost. Village registers tell of the horror, misery and death. In 1630 there were only fifty families left in Löhlbach. In 1640, seven thousand troops marched through Frankenburg and Löhlbach and took horses, cows, sheep, chickens, and all the property from homes they could haul away in wagons. Soldiers destroyed or stole almost everything from Kassel to Marburg. Marburg lost half of its inhabitants.

Czechoslovakia precipitated the Thirty Year's religious war when Lutheran churches were closed in Prague. Lutherans were defeated for a time until Sweden's Lutheran King Gustaf Adolph sent 7,000 soldiers into Germany. France sent soldiers to Germany to defeat the troops from Sweden. The center of Germany was not completely destroyed, but it was impossible to know who was alive and where they had gone. Approximately two thirds of the industrial, agricultural, and commercial facilities of Germany were in ruins. By 1648, Germany's population was reduced to five million people.

The census taken in Germany in 1747 presents the living conditions. How much terror, misery and death are hidden behind the numbers because the Thirty Years War is within this period? It was a time of senseless and atrocious devastation in Europe, connected with an unbelievable diminution of the population. Cities and villages were in ruins and ashes. In 1611, 1624, 1625, and 1635-36 pestilence took many lives. Register entries show all family members, their servants, and maids, and their families were all buried within one week. Many who survived were forced by starvation to leave the area. The flight from approaching enemies, starvation and diseases diminished the population of villages. Though not completely destroyed, nobody could tell who was still alive and where they had gone.

The only authentic statement about the movement of troops through Hessen is from the year 1639, when there was French quartering. In 1640, there was a great starvation in Germany and until 1643 most people, young and old, left because of it. Even in 1661, actually thirteen years after the peace treaty, only one third of the fields of communities were tilled and in January many people had not enough bread in the house. The terrible winter of 1659-60 in Germany was followed by a drought. The great poverty which had not diminished after the war became greater than before and forced quite a number of people to leave their home country.

The Seven Years's War, 1756–1763, involved Germany, Austria, Sweden, England and France for the possession of Silesia. A hard fought struggle, thousands of peasants discovered that potatoes could be left in the fields through winter months and dug up as needed. Potatoes were safe from military requisitioning unless soldiers had time to dig them. Grain had to be harvested and stored in a building where the first foraging troops to arrive could confiscate the entire crop in the name of the King.

It is amazing that the Krug family survived at all because many Sehlen family names which appeared in 1591 are not to be found again. One hundred years after the war Sehlen had not yet again reached its old population numbers. And again there were war cries in Germany. Bound to England by a treaty, Hessen was part of the allied forces with England, Hanover, Prussia, Austria and France. Even though war was waged in Silesia, Hessen country again was a part of the Western battlefield for a long time. The summer of 1760 a French army approached and marched along the old road from Haina across Gmunden, pitched a camp near Oberholzhausen, and devastated all the fields in such a way that not a sheaf of corn remained. The whole area was looted.

The parson reported a strange phenomenon of nature during the night of April 13, 1767: "This night, after twelve, there was a heavy earthquake...what I felt was a strong heave of the ground so that I was thrown high up into the air from my bed. This earthquake was observed especially strong at Kassel, Germany, and even far into Thuringia. At Rotenburg, chimneys fell down. Apparently all the elements had united so that no peace was permitted after the end of the war.

The winter of 1771 was very hard and long. On April 30th the sowing of oats was not yet completed and already on July 24th no more bread could be bought. The following years brought hard winters, storms, floods and rising prices.

In 1773, more people are said to have died than were born in Europe. The Monday before Whitsun a storm devastated Germany with hail as big as pigeon eggs. Then followed such a heat that twenty corn sheaves yielded not more than one and one-half bushels of corn. It is not surprising that the young men of Hessen went voluntarily when recruited for the army.

May 11, 1775 Johann Justus Krug II, son of Johann Justus Krug I and Anna Gertrud nee Möller, was born in Löhlbach House #70, Germany. Children were given the same name as their father at that time to clarify genealogy. At age 29 years Johann Justus Krug II married a Huguenot maiden from the village of Schwabendorf, Germany. Her name was Wilhelmina Kirchner and she descended from Huguenot ancestors who migrated into Hessen, Germany to escape the oppression of Louis XIV after he had revoked the Edict of Nantes. They left France and went to Prussia as Saxony was known at that time.

In 1776, Landgrave Friedrich II, like many other German princes, gave 1,200 Hessian soldiers by treaty to England to fight the Colonists in North America who were struggling for their independence. Among them was Walter Krug's cousin, Hartmann Happel of Sehlen who went over, "when the

English subjects in America had become rebellious" the parson wrote in the Sehlen church register. According to records in Germany, Hartmann Happel survived the war in North America, returned to Germany, and several of his descendants immigrated in later centuries to America.

Andreas Happel was born in Alt Heim, now Altenhaina, and a member of the Löhlbach church where he was joined in marriage to Maria Elizabeth Möller (Moeller in USA). Villagers did not have transportation in those years other than their feet to walk between the villages. The Happel family walked to Löhlbach to church and there Maria Möller and Andreas met and were married. They and their ten children immigrated to Iowa in 1864. Villagers in Germany did not have access to photography and their only photos were taken in Iowa.

Andrew and Marie Moeller Happel

Andrew and Marie's son, Peter Johann Happel, was born n Altenheina Kreiz, Frankenberg, Provin Hessen Naussau, Germany, and came to America in 1864. He married Katharina Elizabeth Werning in Iowa in 1874. Katharina was born in Dankerode-an-der-Fulda, Germany, the daughter of Adam and Jeanette (Brehm) Werniing, and immigrated to Iowa in March 1870.

Peter Happel and Katharine Werning were married July 3, 1874. Their union was blessed with ten children. Eldest daughter, Christina married Henry John Krug, eldest son of John and Katherine (Michel) Krug.

Ten children of Peter and Katharina Happel
Back row: August Anton, Elizabeth Jeanette, Adam Martin, Christina Marie, Maria Elizabeth, Heinrich August, Katharina Wilhelmina
Front row: William Martin, Peter Johann Happel, Andrew Adam, Katharina Elizabeth Werning, Anna Christina Elizabeth

Peter Johann Happel and Katharina Elizabeth Werning

CHAPTER 4
Centuries of Farmers

Generations of the Krug family who immigrated to America were peasants from Hessen Nassau, Prussia, later known as Germany. On the maternal side of the Krug family Walter's mother was born a Happel, also a farming family in Germany originating in Sehlen, a village from ancient years where archeologists unearthed tools that were used to cultivate the soil in the "Bronze Age," 4,000 years ago. Later, the Happel family moved to Alt Heim known today as Altenhaima.

St. Bonifatius brought Christianity to these forefathers. The Kloster Monsastery at Fulda, Germany, records the history there around the time of Charles the Great when a strong border was founded with fortifications to protect lands from the rebellious Saxons.

Walter's father Henry Krug was born seven years after his parents came to America from Löhlbach in the Haina Kloser area of the state of Hessen Nassau. Both of Walter's grandparents came from the same village in Germany. The land either belonged to the nobility or the church at that time in Germany. Farms produced rye, barley, oats and peas. Wheat did not grow well. Due to the "winter-like climate" the rye was always full of weeds and it was very difficult to keep it clean. Hogs in the Haina forests ate acorns and beechnuts.

The Haina Monastery records, handwritten by monks in 1653, show Krugs gave thirty sheaves of sickled grain to the monastery for farming land owned by the monastery, and in 1655 Krugs paid twelve sheaves; in 1657 Krugs gave fifty-nine sickled sheaves; 1660 Krugs paid thirteen sheaves of rye; and in 1680 seven sheaves of rye was given to the monastery for their share of use of the land farmed by Krugs. The land either belonged to the nobility or the church at that time in Germany.

In 1776, Landgrave Friedrich II, like many other German princes, gave twelve-hundred Hessian soldiers by treaty to England to fight the Colonists in North America who were struggling for their independence. Among them was Walter's cousin Hartmann Happpel of Sehlen, Germany who went abroad, "when the English subjects in America had become rebellious" as the parson wrote in the Sehlen church register. According to records in Germany, Hartmann Happel of Sehlen survived the war in North America, returned to Germany, and several of his descendants immigrated in later centuries to America.

The first of Walter's relatives to immigrate to America from Germany, Johann Peter Michel, age twenty-six years, left Bremen, Germany, on the ship *Lima*, arriving in New York July 17, 1857, the same year the Tanner family joined pioneers from Ohio and Michigan in a prairie schooner train to settle on the Great Plains of Iowa. Johann Michel sent a letter to the Krug family in Löhlbach, Germany that President Lincoln signed the Homestead Act to dispurse lands west of the Mississpppi River. The Civil War was raging when the Krug family sold their fachwerk home and store and all their furnishings located on the main street of Löhlbach, as recorded in the Löhlbach church records.

According to the parson of the Löhlbach church, the potato rot disease of Europe devasted the continent at this time and Löhlbachers staple diet was milk and potatoes. Krug ancestors were hungry! It was illegal to take money out of Germany, and it is believed the Krug family smuggled their money out of Germany by the most common method—sewing it into the linings and hems of their clothing as they emigrated.

Five of the Johann Justus Krug III family arrived in New York on the sailing ship *Columbia*, July 19, 1865: Johann Justus III age 59, Anna 54, Elizabeth 24, Johann 21, Heinrich 18. After arrival in America, the Krug family lived their first winter in Iowa with the Michel family on a farm in Fremont Township, Benton County, Iowa. That winter Johann Justus Krug III purchased an eighty acre farm and paid for it with the money from selling their home and possessions in Germany. The church records in Löhlbach, Germany record "the family sold their home and all their possessions and immigrated to America." At that time German money had a strong, favorable exchange rate in USA.

1865 Justus Krug immigration trunk as
it is today on the Krug Iowa farm.

The Prussian War was boiling when the Krug family left Germany. Their oldest son Johann Peter, age 21, would be required to report for compulsory military duty. He was accompanied to Bremen, the departure port, by his parent

Johann Justus III, age 59; and Anna, age 54; sister Elizabeth, age 26, and brother Heinrich, age 19. Another sister and a brother had died at a young age in Germany. The oldest child in the Krug family, daughter Wilhelmina, married widower Georg Moller, and together with his children emigrated from Germany on November 12, 1861 arriving in Iowa February 1, 1862.

In 1868, oldest Krug son Johann Peter married Michel daughter, Anna Katharina, in Iowa. Their oldest son Henry was born seven years after his father arrived in America and he had not yet become an American citizen. Five years of residency was required to file an oath of intention for citizenship and another two years was required before citizenship was granted.

Krug ancestors came from five villages in a six mile area northeast of Marburg, Germany and from Dankerode-an-der-Fulda, a distance of thirty miles from Löhlbach. They were peasants farming the land in Germany owned by the church or the nobility.

PART II

While the earth remaineth, seedtime and harvest, and cold and heat, and summer and winter, and day and night shall not cease. Genesis 8:22

CHAPTER 5
Twentieth Century USA

Henry Krug and Christina Happel Krug owned a car, one of the three cars, parked at St.Stephen's Church every Sunday morning in Fremont Township, Benton County, Iowa, in the early 20th century. The family drove to church, a distance of three and one-half miles from their farm located on U.S. 30 and the Linn-Benton County line, when the sun was shining and the roads were dry. If it rained, the car would slide in the ditch because all the roads were mud at that time. The Krugs bought the car in 1912, a Dreadnaught Moline demonstrator 1911 model with a right hand drive and 1,000 miles when they purchased it. During inclement weather, the family rode to church in a horse and buggy. They never missed Sunday worship service and the opportunity to give thanks to Almighty God for the blessings of a better life in America.

Henry and Christina Krug

Both Henry and Christina Krug were born in the United States of America, the oldest son and the oldest daughter of Löhlbach, Germany emigrants: Johann Peter Krug and Anna Katharina Michel Krug; and, Johann Peter Happel and Katharina Elizabeth Werning Happel. The families continued to speak their native German language through two generations born in America.

Their son Walter Krug learned to drive the Dreadnaught Moline when he was thirteen years old. The crankshaft of the 1911 car backfired when the spark lever was set wrong, made timing wrong, and it threw his wrist out of joint. He and his four siblings rode a horse to school the three and one-half miles from their farm to the Christian Day School located next to the church. They studied all eight grades in the German language and began learning English as a subject in the first grade. English was their second language. Arithmetic was taught only in English. Slates, with lacing around the edges to silence them on the school desk, were used for teaching the Palmer Method of cursive writing. Students daily used a German language hymnal and a German Bible in school.

Walter remembered his shyness and difficulty in learning to speak the English language. The teacher, in his first year of teaching at the school, asked him to pronounce out loud "A"—"ah." Walter responded "Ich can das 'ah' nicht sprechen." He did not realize that he was pronouncing "ah" in the sentence until the teacher became amused at his speech and called attention to his accomplishment.

The advent of the horseless carriage emphasized speed which quickly caught on with German youth in Iowa. There were speeds of forty miles an hour coasting on a sled in wintertime down a hill east of the Krug homestead. School children from the Krug School, Fremont No. 7, slid forty rods at that fast speed.

Walter attended the local public school, located across from the Krug homestead, in winter the first year after he had completed eight grades at the Christian Day School. The Krug public school teacher allowed the students to omit recesses morning and afternoon so they could have a longer noon hour for coasting on the icy road. Walter attended the school all year until May when spring work began on the farm, to learn advanced mathematics because there was not a High School in that part of the county at that time.

In World War I the banks became shaky and Henry and Christina Krug decided to take their money out of the bank and invest it in land. In 1922, they owned two farms. In 1923, they bought a third farm and paid for all of them in cash. In 1930 they bought their last farm.

It was necessary to have large pieces of machinery to operate that much land and beginning in 1922, when Walter was eighteen years old, his Krug parents purchased a 1530 (15 horse power, 30 on the belt) Hart Parr Oliver tractor, corn sheller, three bottom plow and a ten foot tandem disc for $1,350.00. Walter remembered the evening when the farm implement dealer, his Uncle August Happel, came to his parent's farm to write the deal for the tractor, corn sheller, plow, and tandem disc. Uncle August Happel was Walter's baptismal Godfather and gave him his middle name. Uncle August had lost his business in his early years when his business partner hit and killed a little girl and the business was sued, but he paid off his partner's debts and lost his business in the process. He started up in business again and prospered to become Eastern Iowa's largest twentieth century farm implement dealer.

The new machinery made it possible to do custom work as well as the work on the Krug farms. Walter operated the machinery for custom work and left home for as much as a week at a time on jobs shelling corn for people that required him to stay overnight with the family. Rain and muddy roads made it difficult to haul grain and often delayed the shelling process.

In 1924, Henry and Christina Krug purchased a Moline Knight, a seven passenger car with folding jump seats, at a cost of $2,500-$3,000. They also owned a Moline R & V Knight. In October of the same year, they traded in a 1920 Model T Ford and paid an additional $300 for a Model T Ford touring luxury car to give to Walter on his 21st birthday, emancipation year at that time.

In 1925, Henry Krug bought a used threshing machine from his brother-in-law, farm implement dealer August Happel, for $1,000.00. A new machine cost about $1,500.00 in those days. Henry Krug used the threshing machine until 1938 with a "threshing ring" of his four sons and their neighbors.

Corn was harvested by hand in the early years of the 20th century. The Krug family went out with two, three or four wagons into a field, depending upon the number of pickers and horses to help. Warm autumn weather was of much benefit in that it dried the fields and corn and made husking easier. A husking hook was used on the right hand to easily free the corn ear from the stalk. Walter and his sister Emma husked three rows of corn between them. One person working alone took two rows of corn at a time. As soon as one load was filled, Emma helped fill another wagon. A Michel cousin worked for the family picking corn for a dollar a day, one cent a bushel, when Henry Krug ran a sliver in his hand that became badly infected and he could not pick corn that season. The Michel cousin also did the chores in the evening without extra pay. Christina Krug patched his mittens and repaired his clothes because he could not buy new clothing on the amount of money he was paid for helping with the corn harvest.

Walter's family finished picking corn on Armistice Day of World War I. His mother heard over the telephone party line that the war was over and that people were celebrating. Life was much less eventful in those years. The only communication was the party line telephone. "Ver sind mir zu hein ge stayen." Translation: We stayed home more.

Farm living for the Krug family in the early years of the 20th century had few leisure moments for either parents or children. Henry Krug, a skilled carpenter and farmer, supervised his four sons in farming, building chicken houses, machine sheds, hog sheds, corn cribs, cattle sheds, milk sheds, wood sheds, anything needed on the farm, and the repairing of farm buildings on land owned by the family and on the farms of Henry's five brothers.

When time permitted, and a carpenter crew was needed to build retirement homes for his relatives, Henry Krug worked with the carpentry crew. He helped build three large homes for retiring farmers in the rural town of Atkins in the early years of the century. Henry Krug was the oldest son of imigrant parents who had ten children, the six sons were all farmers. He was sent in his youth by his parents to a St. Louis trade school to learn carpentry skills. His parents, from Germany, realized the lack of buildings on Iowa prairie farms at that time and knew carpentry skills were greatly needed.

Immigrant Johann Justus Krug III and his wife Anna Elisabeth nee Paar paid $400 for their eighty acre homestead along U.S. 30 in Fremont Township, Benton County in 1866. They later purchased another eighty acres for a total of 160 acres. Oldest son John Peter and his wife Anna Katharina nee Michel lived with them on the homestead and had eleven children, including one set of twins. Six sons and four daughters survived. A grandson of John Peter and Anna Katharina continued to live on the Krug homestead and a large celebration was held at the farm in the 21st century on the 150th year date of the family's arrival on that farm in America.

Celebration of the Krug family in Iowa,
150 years living on the same farm

Walter remembered using his father's carpentry tools, his keyhole saw, when he was nine years old to cut circles of wood into wagon wheels. He also made box traps to catch wild rabbits, and made boxes to raise young pigeons in the hog house, the cattle shed, and the enclosed peak of the chicken house where he made compartment nests and landing board slots for the flock of wild pigeons which numbered as many as one-hundred at a time. From inside the buildings he made doors that opened up and the pigeon boxes could then be cleaned. There were also pigeon nests in the cupola of the barn and in the garage. Some pigeons were white with red eyes, some gray, some brown, and a mixture of all three colors; some were a light blue. The pigeons climbed in and out of the opening of the wooden carrier track in the haymow of the barn. They ate loose grain or corn around the hog pen and livestock feed bunks in the barnyard. They nested on ledges in the barn and on any place that was four inches wide.

During summer nesting they had as many as four or five hatchings.

When there was a large flock of pigeons they would all fly up as a flock and make a large noise. Walter remembered shooting into the flock with a shotgun to thin them out. Christina Krug made Tauben Soup (translation: squab soup) from the young squabs when they were just ready to fly. She cleaned three young squabs each time and soaked them in cold water for at least one-half hour before chilling them overnight. The next day she boiled them in three quarts of water with a tablespoon of salt until the meat was tender. The liquid was set aside to cool and one cup of rice cooked in it until tender. The squab meat was cut into small pieces and added to the rice along with two beaten eggs and a cup of sweet cream.

The farm Henry and Christina Krug bought on U.S. 30, located along the Linn-Benton County line, was an "improved farm" with electricity, indoor plumbed washroom on the first floor, and full bathroom with tub, sink and toilet on the second floor. It had been a berry farm and the previous owners marketed berries in the city of Cedar Rapids, Iowa. There were still plenty of berries for picking during the summer months and the five Krug children sold them at the farmer's market in Cedar Rapids. They were assigned to keep the ripe berries picked all summer long and many were needed for baking berry pies, as many as five pies a day in the summer season. There was always pie for family meals, relative company, and for extra farm laborers. Favorite pies were raspberry, gooseberry and rhubarb combined with elderberries and currents. Christina Krug also made chocolate, lemon, custard, and open-faced apple pies all year long. Three kinds of dessert—pie, cake and fruit were regularly served at meals for laborers and guests.

In winter, when farm work slowed and it snowed, the Krug sons went rabbit hunting with ferrets. They had one ferret at home, a female, which they bred. They also bought several ferrets and fed them milk and meat, and rabbit-heads. They were tame and knew their master and did not bite. Rabbits were caught and frozen with the skins on, then sold to a butcher for twenty-five cents each. To increase the number of rabbits caught, the ferrets were not fed so they would work better. Ferrets were harnessed and kept on a leash when put in groundhog holes to scare the rabbits out for shooting. Several times a ferret stayed in a rabbit hole because the string-like leash broke. If the leash became caught in a hole, a ferret would die if it wasn't freed. When there wasn't too much frost in the ground, it was possible to dig out a ferret stuck in a hole with a crowbar and spade. If there was a rabbit in the hole, the ferret would catch the rabbit and eat it, go to sleep and never come out. If the frost had frozen the ground so hard it was not possible to dig, the hole was plugged up and the Krug boys went back several days later to try to catch the ferret.

A favorite and long remembered ferret of Walter and his brothers was "Minnie." She broke away one day and stayed in a hole. She was gone for several weeks. One cold winter morning a neighbor saw something coming down the ice covering the creek and stopped his horse and sled to go down to the creek and see what it was. Sure enough, he caught "Minnie" still wearing the harness and string leash, and returned her to the Krug boys.

Rabbit was an important part of the Krug diet in winter. Christina Krug cut up the rabbits and dipped them into flour and salt, pepper to taste, then browned them on the stove. She added water to the skillet and made gravy when they finished cooking. Sometimes rabbits were left whole, filled with bread stuffing, and baked in the oven. Walter continued to trap rabbits all his life and always enjoyed eating them. He moved his most often used trap to Atkins when he retired in his newly built home and continued trapping in winter in his backyard garden. His grandson now owns his rabbit trap.

Walter often remembered that the orange found in the sack of nuts and candy given to the children in his youth after

Christmas Eve services at the church was the only time during the year he had citrus fruit to eat, a rare treat. He did not have a Christmas tree at home though Christmas was celebrated by going to church services where there was a decorated and lighted tree for three days each year. When Walter was ten years old, before World War I, he wanted a trimmed tree in his farm home so much that he climbed the tallest spruce tree in their farm grove and cut the top out of it. It was the first time the Henry Krug family ever had a decorated Christmas tree in their farm home.

Christina Krug sewed all the clothing for her growing family. A photograph was taken by a traveling photographer in 1915 of Henry and Christina Krug's family on the farm showing the five children in everyday clothing. It is noticeable that all the family was wearing their mother's homemade garments. She even knitted stockings for the family, cotton for summer and wool to wear in the winter.

The five children of Henry and Christina Krug in clothing made by their mother: Walter, Gerhardt, Emma, Clarence, and Arthur

Henry and Christina Krug spoke High German, their first language, though they were bilingual. They attended a German speaking Christian Day school and studied English as a subject in school. In their private life they spoke their native German language for more easily understood expressions, and when they were in public and meeting people of other nationalities they spoke the English language.

On Friday, March 9, 1923 Henry and Christina Krug celebrated their 25th Silver Wedding Anniversary with a reception in their farm home for all their family including all their siblings and their families. Rev. G. Rickels, pastor of St. Stephen's Lutheran Church, gave a sermon in the German language:

Geliebte Freunde:

Ihr habt heute ein Freudenfest veranstaltet, ein Fest da ihr die Gelegenheit wahrnehmen wollet, eurem Gotte Dank zu opfern und mit euren Freunden froehlich zu sein. Der Anlass hierzu ist der 25ste Wiederkehr eures Hochzeitstages.

Dazu habt ihr hohe Ursashe; denn es ist doch eine grosse Gnade Gottes, fuenf-und-zwanzig Jahre glueskieb im heilgen Ehestande zu leben. Solches ist euch von Gott dem Herrn vergoeunt worden. Dass Gott euch im den verflossenen Jahren gesegnet hat, ist offenbar. Er hat euch mehr gesegnet, als ihr einst am eurem ersten Hochzeitstages hoffen durftet. Darum habt ihr heute wirklicn Ursashe froehlich und dankbar zu sein.

Lasset mich euch nun kurz zeigen, was der eigentliche Ursprung eurer Freude an diesem Tage sein sollte. Ganz kurz gesagt: Fs ist die

Gnade Gottes, die also gross und dauerud ist, wie sie im unserm Texte beschrieben wird. Um die Groesse der Gnade Gottes im das rechte Liebt zu stellen, wollen wir einmal die Kehrseite betrachten und sehen, was ihr ohne die Gnade Gottes gewesen waeret. Gesetzt ihr haettet in den verflossenen Jahren die Gnade Gottes nicht genossen, was dann?

Sehet, wir sind Suender, und wenn Gott nicht gnaedig waere, dann muesste er uns zuernen. Dann koennte er uns nicht lieben, kein Gutes tun. Da Werk unserer Haende waere vergebliche Muehe; es waere kein Vorwaertskommen. Wir heatlen wohl keine Gesundheit und keinen Trost im Krankheit. Was sollte uns dann Mut und Kraft geben im Anfeshtung und Widerwaertigkeit? Trostlos waere unser Leben und mit Furcht erfuellt vor dem Zorne Gottes.

Aber nun ist Gottes Gnade vorhanden gewesen, anhaltend und reichlich. Ja, wir wissen, die Gnade Gottes ist immerwaebrend. Und durch diese Gnade Seid Ihr reichlich gesegnet worden. Er hat euch im irdischen wohl versogt. Auf Das Werk eurer Haende hat Gottes Segen geruht. Er hat Euch ein gutes friedliches heim bescheert. Gott hat euch eine Feine Familie gegben, daran ihr eure Freude habt, die euch ein Trost und ein Beistand ist, ein herrliches Gnadengeschenk Gottes.

Aber noch grossere Gnade ist es, dass er euch bei der Erkenntnis seiner Gnade erhalten hat. Er hat euch immerzu sein Wort bescheert, daraus ihr alle Tage erkennen konntet, dass er gnaedig ist und, warum er gnaedig ist, naehmlich um seines lieben Sohnes Jesu Christi willen.

Fuenf-und-zwanzig Jahre vom Mannesalter sind nun vergangen. Da sind doch wohl die besten Jahre dahin, und mit rasehen Sehritten kommt das Alter, die Tage, von denen wir sagen, sie gefallen uns nicht. Was wird dann werden? Muss man nicht mit Bangigkeit in die Zukunft sehausen?

Sehet, im Texte ist Trost vorhanden. Es sollen wohl Berge weichen und Huegel hinfallen. Also, wenn auch so grosses Unglueck kommt, so soll Gottes Gnade doch noch bleiben. Und so arg wird es dochnicht werden. Also, die Gnade Gottes ist uns immer zugesagt. Einerleil was kommen mag, Gott will uns gnaedig sein, ommt Widerwaertigkeit, Gott ist bei uns mit seiner Gnade; kommt Krankheit, Gott is bei uns mit seiner Gnade; kommen die Gebrechliehkeiten des Alters, so ist doch Gott mit uns mit seiner Liebe und seiner Barmherzigkeit. Ja, kommt auch endlich die Zeit der Trenrung, da Gott selber den Ehebund aufhebt, und das Herz mit grosser Trauer erfuellt ist, auch dann noch will Gott mit uns sein mit seiner Gnade.

Und ist er bei uns mit seiner Gnade, dann kann uns kein Feind schaden. Der Teufel hat dann keine Macht mehr, auch der Tod hat seinen Stachel verloren, und nach einer kurzen Ruhe gibt es ein froehliches Wiedersehen in der ewigen Seligkeit.

Diese Verheissung Gottes ist euch geredet. Daran haltet euch, und freuet euch, und danket Gott fuer diese Gnade, so wird Gott euch auch in

kuenftigen Jahren Glueck und Segen geben, wie er im den vergangenen Jahren getan hat.
Lieder.
> 346
> 341 v.3.
> 4 & 5.

Translation:

Dear Friends,

You are gathered here today with your friends for a celebration and to take this opportunity to offer your thanks to God. The reason is the 25th Anniversary of your wedding day.

You have good reason because it is by the great Grace of God twenty-five years have passed in happy holy matrimony. Such was granted to you by Lord God. That God blessed you in the past years is obvious. He has blessed you more than you were allowed to hope for on your wedding day. Therefore, you really have reason today to be happy and thankful.

Let me now show you briefly what the actual origin of your joy should be on this day. Briefly stated, it is the Grace of God, which is great and eternal as it is described in our scriptures.

To put the greatness of God's Grace in the right light, we want to look at the reverse—what you would have been without the Grace of God. In other words, what would have happened over the years if you had not enjoyed the Grace of God; what then?

Look at it, we are sinners, and if God were not gracious, then he would have to be wrathful. Then He could not love us, and could not do good. The work of our hands would be futile; there would be no progress. We would have no health and no comfort in sickness. What then would give us the courage and strength to resist discouragement? It would be a life without comfort and filled with the fear of God's wrath.

But instead, here was the hand of God's Grace—eternal and abundant. Yes, we know! God's Grace is everlasting. And by this Grace you were richly blessed. He has taken care of you well in this world. God's blessing has rested on the work of your hands. He has bestowed to you a good and peaceful home. God gave you a fine family which gives you joy, which gives you comfort; which gives you support; so generous is God's Grace.

Even greater is the grace that He has kept you with that knowledge. He has always bestowed His word on you through which you could know He is gracious and why He is gracious, through the will of his beloved son Jesus Christ.

Twenty-five years of human age has passed. There went the best years; and with fast steps comes old age—the days which we dislike. What will come then? Must one see the future with worry?

In the scriptures there is comfort. Mountains may give way and hills may fall, even when catastrophe comes, God's Grace remains. God's Grace is always promised to us. Regardless of what will come, God will be gracious to us. If discouragement comes; God will be with us with his Grace; if sickness comes; God will be with us with His Grace; when the feebleness of old age comes; God will be with us with His love and compassion (mercy). Yes, if the time of parting comes, where God Himself lifts the wedding vows, and the heart is filled with great sorrow, then also God will be with us with His Grace.

And if He is with us with His Grace, then no enemy can hurt us. The devil has no power, and death has lost its sting, and after a short stillness there will be a joyous meeting in everlasting life.

This is God's promise to you. Observe this promise, and be happy, and thank God for this Grace; God will grant you in the coming years abundant blessings as he did in the past years.

The hard work ethic brought from Germany in the 19th century continued in descendants in the 20th century. They valued and saved the money they earned. Walter said of his parents, "They still have the first dime they ever earned." Enid summed it up when she said, "Every penny counts in your Krug family." It was a sore point with Enid. She detested Walter counting every postage stamp she bought and used to order flowers for her hobby of growing and exchanging "slips" by mail with other flower hobbyists.

The 120 acre farm Walter and Enid Krug lived on, purchased by Henry and Christina Krug from a first cousin had been continuously owned by the Krug family from the time Henry Krug's Aunt Wilhelmina and Uncle George Möller (Moeller in USA) imigrated from Germany in 1862. Walter Krug took possession of the land for his Krug parents on March 1, 1931.

Henry and Christina Krug paid in cash for farms they bought during this time of the Great Depression when many people had little or no money. They raised a lot of corn, oats, cattle and hogs on 580 acres of rich farmland they owned in Linn and Benton Counties, all within four miles of rural Atkins. They had four sons to help them in farming

Both Henry and Christina Krug were born in Fremont Township, Benton County Iowa. Christina never traveled more than thirty miles away from the place of her birth during her entire lifetime though she lived on three farms and had many relatives on farms that she often visited. She was a midwife in the Happel family and even delivered her own children.

"My mother and I were the only ones present the day I was born," Walter said all the years of his life. It was the second day of August and his father was threshing oats away from their home at the time of his birth, therefore, his mother delivered him without assistance. He was her fourth child, the first two children having been twins.

Christina Happel Krug grew up in neighboring Eldorado Township. She and Henry Krug's acquaintance blossomed when they attended joint church youth group meetings. After marriage, Christina Krug was president of St. Stephens Ladies Society, the Frauen Verein. She conducted their meeting one March afternoon and returned to the farm to the chicken yard to chase down and butcher a chicken for dinner that evening. In the night she had a stroke. Henry Krug phoned Dr. Bradley who came immediately to their home, but she did not live until morning.

When the cattle did not behave or something went wrong with the animals, Walter spoke loudly in the German language, words yelled so fast only guttural sounds were audible. When he was angry or roiled about the livestock, he might have been cursing in Germany, but it was impossible to know because Walter never cursed in the English language.

Walter and all of his relatives formed a coalition to prevent the younger generation from learning the German language. If any of his family noticed the youger generation listening to them speaking in German, they stopped talking and chastened, "You don't speak German. You speak English!"

"German will never do you any good in your lifetime," Walter said. He belonged to the Americanization generation of his family. The drive to banish all things associated with Old World culture dominated his life.

When Congress passed legislation during World War I to ban the teaching of the German language in schools of the country, the predominantly German community banned together to make sure the younger generation spoke only English as a first language. Children were not permitted to have anything with Gothic lettering on it or to learn anything about Grimms Fairy Tales. Children were not told that Gothic lettering is predominant in Germany, and that Krug family heritage villages were near Kassel, Germany where the Brothers Grimm were librarians and wrote the fairy tales. It was years before this could be discovered in travel to Germany.

A few German words slipped into everyone's vocabulary. Everyone in all the German families was permitted to say "Dankeschön" when hearing someone say "Gesundheit" after a sneeze. Enid frequently used the German word "heiss" spoken with a sizzling sound which she preferred when something was hot to teach everyone to be careful. It was the only German word Enid ever spoke.

"There is always a relative standing on your porch interrupting mealtime hours to talk with your father," Grandma Inez Bryner observed when she visited the farm. Grandma was right. There was always one of father's brothers or uncles on the back porch of the house at mealtime to talk over the next day of farm work during the years of the extended family farm operation. Meals were the time of day when they could talk over their work plans.

"Your mother works harder than I ever had to when I lived on a farm," Grandma Inez said. Grandma was right. Mother spent all her time preparing food for the next meal and to ensure enough for extra workers at the table, also enough for a "covered dish" to take for potluck at every meeting she attended away from home. She was always chasing a chicken to catch and kill for meals or planting, cultivating or harvesting food in her garden that needed preparation before mealtime.

The harvest season was a time when Grandpa Henry Krug and father's brothers were frequent guests at meals in our home. The men relaxed together over the meal table. They were hearty eaters of more than one serving of the main course and of several desserts. This gave them time to talk together which they often had little time for when they were working. It was the only time their conversations could be heard in both German and English, though only they could understand the German language.

The Thanksgiving prayer was always given by Grandpa Henry Krug at the end of the meal in the German language. When he was not present at a meal, an uncle prayed the prayers. Walter, my father, translated them for me and found great joy in discovering the English speaking generation was interested in knowing what had been prayed over the years in the homes of our extended family:

> We thank Thee, dear Lord Jesus
> That thou our Guest has been;
> O be thou with us ever
> And save us from all sin. Amen

> We thank Thee Lord
> For meat and drink
> Through Jesus Christ. Amen

We thank Thee for these gifts, O Lord;
Pray feed our souls, too, with Thy Word.
Amen

O give thanks unto the Lord, for he is
good; for his mercy endureth forever. Amen

Heavenly Father, accept our thanks for this
food and for all They blessings through
Jesus Christ. Amen

Thanks be unto Thee, O God. Amen

    German families liked home canned Concord grape juice and homemade root beer as refreshing drinks to enjoy or serve socially when company arrived at any time during the year. Root Beer Extract was purchased, made into a drink and bottled by home methods. Bottles were reused year after year and capped with a simple machine. Cakes of yeast dissolved in a little sugar in a pint of lukewarm water, were left to set in a warm place for twelve hours, then stirred and strained through cheese-cloth. A bottle of Root Beer Extract was added along with four pounds of sugar and five gallons of lukewarm water. The mixture was bottled and kept in a warm place for forty-eight hours. After cooling it was ready for capping and kept well in the cellar at low temperature. Sometimes root beer continued to "work" after it was capped and the bottles would blow their tops. Opened bottles had too yeasty a flavor for pleasant drinking. A successful batch that did not "work" after it was bottled and capped or did not taste of yeast was especially satisfying, and was a treat to enjoy.
    In German-American families it was traditional for the bride's parents to furnish furniture and a stove for cooking; the groom's parents furnished the animals for farming. Grandma Groff raised Enid and did not go for the idea of furnishing the

cook stove. She insisted Walter buy the stove for their home so he drove a team and wagon to a hardware store in Cedar Rapids and bought a "Quick Meal" cook stove, with "chickens running after a worm," saying on it and a warming oven on top and a reservoir for water in back. It weighed 300-400 pounds and cost a little over $110.00. Walter every so often reminded everyone that he had purchased the stove.

Walter and Enid's farming years in American: up from small beginnings to greater enterprise. In 1925, the year they married, Walter worked for his parents on their 200 acre Fremont Township, Benton County farm for wages of $500 a year plus a house to live in, a cow to milk, one-hundred laying hens, and a garden. Walter raised one litter of hogs and butchered two of the hogs for food. His parents owned all the cattle on the farm. When it was time to butcher, a quarter of beef was given to Walter and Enid to work up for their meat supply.

Walter's older brother, three years his senior, lived with them to help with farming the large 200 acres with horses and he was paid wages by his parents. Walter's brother also taught Enid how to cook since she had never learned to cook while growing up in her grandmother's home. Her grandparents put silver braces on her teeth to straighten them, gave her organ music lessons, and sent her to Coe College. When she married and moved to this farm home, her grandparents gave her a piano and stool for her home.

After five years of farming the 200 acres, Walter's older brother, who lived and farmed with him, planned to marry. Walter's oldest brother moved onto the 200 acre farm, and Enid and Walter moved to Cedar Rapids for one year. They took their chickens to the city and also raised a garden at their home on Johnson Avenue West that they rented for $360.00 for the year. The Krug grandparents continued to pay Walter $500 a year wages for working on their farms.

While living in Cedar Rapids, Walter met the owner of a nearby DX gas service station located a few blocks from their Johnson Ave. home. Walter worked in the station for $1.00 a day and $1.00 a night pumping gas, changing oil, and washing cars. The station was not too busy during 1930, but it was possible to earn extra cash working there during the Great Depression days. Sometimes a traveling man stopped at the station and needed a bedroom to sleep in and his car washed. Walter and Enid earned $3.00 extra money for providing the needed bedroom and car wash.

In 1930, Henry and Christina Krug bought a 120 acre farm for $240 an acre for Walter to farm. Walter and Enid moved onto the farm March 4-5, 1931 taking possession of it for their parents and paid them seven dollars an acre rent each year for the farm.

The Great Depression was hitting hard at the time. Part of the original house on the farm, built in the 1800's, had been preserved and moved to a new cement foundation on the west edge of the barnyard when the new farmhouse was built in 1905. Square nails and hand sawed lumber were characteristics of the "old house" early day construction. It was used as a chicken house for laying hens, a calf barn, and later became a storage place for lumber, and a place to raise domestic rabbits.

The spring of 1931, Walter bought a Model T Grinder to saw wood to stoke the wood furnace in the house. A governor was put on the motor to saw wood. The grinder was also used to grind sausage when Henry Krug's recipe, using both beef and pork, was made into the traditional family sausage stuffed casings that were then smoked in the smokehouse on the farm. The Model T chassis, drive shaft taken out, had a feeder grinder mounted on it.

Walter finished putting in the last rows of corn by May 15th, the time to complete corn planting to ensure its maturity by September 15th, the end of the ninety day growing season. He eagerly watched for the first planted corn coming up to "row" it both ways across the field. He watched the blossoms on the lilac bushes that opened at the same time in May, comparing how heavy the lilacs bloomed with previous years, a sign to predict in advance as he had been taught by a neighbor in his youth before the use of fertilizer and hybrid seed corn.

Economically it was one of the worst periods in USA's history. Crops in the prairie country were failing, the government had halted the production of money, and banks were failing. The farm house, a five bedroom square frame two-story home, painted white was built in 1905.

It was hot the summer of 1931. June temperatures were in the high 90's F. and low 100's F. with 100% humidity. The temperatures were so high that because of heat exhaustion of the horses it was necessary to cultivate corn in the moonlight after supper. Henry Krug gave his son Walter the seed corn and seed oats to start his first crops in 1931. The corn made forty-five bushels an acre that year. In 1931, the price of corn was only fifteen cents a bushel, oats was eight cents a bushel and my father did not sell the corn or oats crops until 1933. At that time, he needed $75.00 to pay for a side rake so he sold four hundred bushels of corn in May and also had to pay the cost of transporting the corn. Later in the summer, the price rose to fifty cents a bushel and he sold 1,500 bushels of corn.

Hogs sold for $2.45 a hundred pounds or $1.00 a pound for packing hogs. Walter sold old brood sows weighing 300 pounds for one cent a pound or $3.00 for each sow. He sent a whole truck load of brood sows to the Cedar Rapids market and the check for the load was about $70.00.

Fat cattle sold for six cents and seven sents a pound during this time. Eggs were sold at a grocery store for eight cents a dozen. A box of oatmeal cost twenty-one cents. Taxes in 1931 were $1.50 an acre. In 1971 taxes were $10.00 an acre on the same farm.

The story of a South Dakota farmer in the "Great Depression" was told that he sent his sheep to the Chicago stock yards to market and the commission man sent him a bill. He owed them money. The farmer sent word to Chicago that he could not send them any money, but he could send them more sheep.

CHAPTER 6
Prairie Life

Walter and Enid Krug started farming with six cows to milk that were given to them by the Krug parents, and four horses bought from the gas station owner Walter worked for in Cedar Rapids. The owner was dissolving a farm he owned and sold the horses. Walter's father also gave them another team of horses, three or four brood sows, at least one hundred fifty laying hens besides they had quite a few they had raised while they lived in Cedar Rapids. Walter often ground feed for the chickens at his parent's farm and they would tell him to fill up some sacks with feed to take home to his chickens.

To start farming, $200-$300 worth of machinery was needed. Walter bought a new John Deere harrow for $45.00 from a salesman who was a former student of Enid's mother Inez Bryner. This same harrow sold for $18.00 at Walter's farm auction when he retired from farming in February 1966.

Henry Krug sold his son his triple-box wagon which he had purchased in 1918 when Walter was thirteen years old. At a farm sale Walter bought a Champion six-foot binder for $2.50. Walter and his brother, who lived on the next farm, cut their oats for three years with the binder. During World War II Walter dismantled the old Champion binder and sold the iron in it for the war effort.

At another farm sale Walter bought a John Deere two bottom plow, called a gang plow for $16.50-$17.00 and a Corn King Manure spreader for $3.50. He also purchased a walking cultivator with two shovels on each side for $4.00-$5.00. It was already an antique piece of machinery at that time. A team was hitched to the cultivator, but it was operated by hand and Walter used it for cultivating potatoes. In World War II Walter dismantled it and sold the iron for the war effort. He also sold scrap iron from the Moline riding cultivator that his father bought in 1923 and sold to him for $25.00.

At a farm sale Walter bought a used oats seeder for $10.00. With two horses, three corn rows could be seeded at a time. Walter and his brother, who farmed on the next farm, used this seeder every year until Walter bought an ingate seeder that fit on the back end of the wagon and the seed came off the wagon onto the whirling action of the seeder. An ingate seeder could sow a twenty acre field in two to two and one-half hours.

A wind storm the first day of September 1931 blew the large cupola off the barn. The old nails gave "away". The barn was built in 1910 and the wind was so strong it blew the top off the straw stack, the straw still dry from threshing because of lack of rain. Henry Krug not only owned the farm, he had insurance on all the farm buildings. He collected insurance for the loss of the cupola and bought and installed a new metal cupola on the barn. He then came to our farm and rebuilt the old wooden cupola into a bigger goose house. It sat in the house yard until my mother insisted it be moved into the orchard because the geese were chasing everyone who went out of the house. Geese made a commotion whenever anyone came onto the farm. They were cheap to feed because they ate grass, and provided good holiday fare when stuffed and roasted for dinner. The geese chased children playing so often that Enid finally got rid of all of the geese.

The drought year 1934 there were many grasshoppers because there was no rain until the 4th of July. Lack of rain in summer when grasshopper eggs are hatching makes them abundant. Grasshoppers chewed the husks off the corn ears, and stunted the corn stalks when the leaves were chewed off. The worst grasshopper year was when alfalfa was chewed off and grasshoppers almost chewed up the corn fields.

Potatoes were planted on the farm on Good Friday, if the weather permitted. It depended upon the rainfall of the season, and the size of the potatoes how much the crop produced. Some years there were potatoes to sell and some years potatoes had to be purchased. When there was a large crop, Enid made potato pancakes and used more potatoes.

When the potato crop failed, due to drough, it was necessary to buy potatoes. Every year about a sixteenth of an acre of a field plowed, disked, and harrowed was saved to plant to potatoes next to the fence in the field closest to the farm buildings where it was convenient for harvesting them when it was that time. That amount of land would produce a crop of fifty to sixty bushels of potatoes in a normal growing season. Potatoes were selected from the previous year's crop stored in the house basement, and cut up to prepare the seed for planting. The potatoes were cut into pieces, each piece having an 'eye.' Two or more bushel baskets were filled with cut potato seed, after the pieces were dusted with insect repellent, before they were hand planted in the field in rows far enough apart for cultivation with a team of horses.

Potato plants grew fast in hot, humid Iowa summer weather. "Get those little bit of devils!" Walter demanded when potato bugs began striping the plant leaves, devouring them and causing them to die. As soon as children were old enough to walk and carry a small pail it was an assigned chore to walk along the rows of potato plants and hand pick or knock potato bugs off into the pail. Walter sprayed for little bugs under the leaves; sometimes the leaves were picked and put in a bucket, or the nests of eggs on the leaves were squeezed to prevent them from hatching. Potato bugs hatched out in three or four days in hot, humid summer weather. That dreaded annual job on the farm was never forgotten and the family also never forgot to be thankful for food during the Great Depression drought years, remembering that farmers were better off than hungry city folk standing in food lines because they had nothing to eat. Walter and Enid's family consumed two bushels of potatoes a month. Potatoes and milk were the staple diet of the Krug family in Germany before immigration to Iowa. Potatoes remained very important in the USA Krug family diet in the 20th century.

The smaller potatoes were fed to the chickens. The laying hens in the flock liked to eat warm cooked potatoes in cold Iowa weather. Sometimes whole oats was cooked with potato peelings and small potatoes in wintertime, and then fed to the chickens with ground corn and oats. Christina Krug bought a red powder called "Panacea" and added it to cooked potatoes to keep chickens healthy in cold weather. Nearly every cold weather day Walter placed fresh straw on the chicken house floor so the flock could scratch for exercise because laying hens laid more eggs with exercise.

The Krug parents gave Walter and Enid laying hens when they were first married. They washed the eggs and sold them to Enid's relatives and their neighbors in the city of Cedar Rapids who appreciated farm fresh eggs and paid up to 55 cents a dozen for them. Unfortunately, there were not a large number of eggs to sell at that time.

In the Great Depression of 1931 and 1932, egg prices were .07 and .08 cents a dozen. Egg prices did not rise to any great extent until World War II when three or four cases a week, thirty dozen eggs in a case, brought 40 cents a dozen when marketed in Cedar Rapids. The eggs were graded large, medium, small and checks at market time. Regular runs from the farm graded twenty-seven or twenty-eight dozen large eggs, with a couple dozen medium or small eggs a week.

Walter made laying mash for the chicken flock out of ground corn, ground oats, and a 25-35% concentrates mixture of proteins, vitamins, and minerals. He had a platform scale in the corncrib that weighed to 850 pounds. It had a fifty pound scale balancer. When set at zero the balancer checked fifty pounds. There were also 100 pound weights. In later years, the elevator at Atkins ground corn, oats, and mixed the concentrate used on the farm.

Fifty pound bags of ground oyster shell chips were purchased from a feed company elevator. The chickens ate oyster shells for calcium, needed when confined and laying eggs every day. Good laying hens lay a little over two hundred days a year. When laying hens started to complete their yearly cycle, they began laying medium and small size eggs and started into a molt. Molting lasted for sixty days with a loss of feathers, weight gain, and growth of new feathers. The chickens did not all molt at the same time. Extreme hot weather and extreme cold weather slowed down the molting process. In the hot, humid weather of summer the hens went into a molt and they quit laying eggs. Two year old hens quit laying eggs in the hot summer months and did not lay eggs again until the following February. Hens that were one year old continued to lay eggs all year long when given good care.

The chicken flock was expected to be in 60-70 percent production. In cold weather the chickens utilized most of their feed for warmth and they laid few eggs. They laid better when drinking warm water so Walter carried warm water to them twice a day in cold weather. Double yolk eggs caused chickens to rupture. Excited hens laid a blood spot in the egg.

Nests and roosts in the chicken house were sprayed quite often for mites that came from the English sparrows that frequented the chicken pens, hog and cattle yards to pick up loose grain in feed areas. When the bottoms of the roosts filled with mites it was time to spray the chicken house. Walter used dip with water or crank-case oil to spray. He also placed ashes from the house wood furnace in a box in the chicken house for the chickens to dust themselves for mites. After the oil furnace was installed in the house, agricultural lime was placed in the box for the chickens to dust in. In later years, a Malathyon louse powder was used for that purpose.

A kerosene lamp heated the chicken water fountain in the cold of winter, but this increased the danger of fire in the straw used on the floor for chickens to scratch in for exercise. In winter, chickens were fed ear corn when confined. In summer, the chickens were allowed to run around the corn crib to pick up shelled corn as it spilt from the cattle and hog feeders. The chickens that ran loose made nests in the straw pile located near the farm buildings, and also nested under the corn crib, in the cattle shed, in the barn, in the hog house, in the hay mow, and wherever animals were fed grain. To gather eggs and make the rounds of all the nests each night meant climbing over barnyard fences and up the ladder to the hay mow to gather eggs.

Enid raised baby chicks to keep the laying flock replenished yearly. In the 1920's and 1930's this was accomplished with setting hens. Ten to twenty cluck hens from the flock were selected at a time, and set with fifteen eggs apiece in nests made on the dirt floor of the chicken house. Nests were partitioned with pieces of stove wood and a wooden bushel basket or box placed over each hen to cause the hen to start setting. Hens set best if they were removed at night from the chicken house for placement in individual setting nests.

Once a day the boxes were taken off the setting hens long enough so the hens could eat feed and drink water. Enid candled the eggs to see if they were going to hatch by placing them in warm water. If the egg wiggled, it was fertile. She held them up to a light in a hole in a box and if the egg was dark it was fertile. If light showed through the egg, it was not fertile. She removed eggs that were not fertile so the hens did not sit for weeks on eggs that would never hatch. It took three weeks for the eggs to hatch.

Hens with baby chicks were moved to individual coops in the orchard. As the chickens grew, roosters were counted and those deemed extra in the flock appeared on the Sunday dinner menu. Only one rooster was kept in the flock for every 25-30 hens. About two hundred hens and not more than eight to ten roosters made up the flock. Henry Krug built little chicken coops and Enid put setting hens on nests of eggs in the orchard coops to hatch geese, ducks, and Bantam chickens. She enjoyed watching new hatchlings grow and did not seem to mind the additional work feeding and watering the setting hens in the coops.

In the late 1930's and 1940's, 250 hatchery straight-run (both sexes) baby chicks were purchased every spring. A kerosene brooder stove was used in a brooder house to keep the chicks warm. One time the brooder stove started on fire and Walter put it out on the roof of the brooder house.

Chicken hawks and crows were predators of baby chickens on Iowa farms. Chicken hawks are carnivorous with a wing spread of two feet. They swooped down on the orchard chicken coops or the chicken yard and snatched chickens. Chicken hawks and crows nested in the non-deciduous trees in the grove next to the cattle yard, and they nested across the road from the farm in the neighbor's grove of trees. The crows ate both corn and meat and killed baby chickens to drag them to their nests to feed their young birds. Walter hid in the cattle shed next to the grove on our farm and shot with his gun into the flock of crows.

Flocks of blackbirds and starlings also nested in the groves. The blackbirds ripped corn ears open and ate the milk out of the corn when it was still in the husk. Starlings raided and killed other baby birds and threw their eggs out of the nests, but mostly they were grain and worm eaters.

There were many pigeons in a flock that lived in the farm barn. They were the wild variety—white with red eyes, gray, brown, mixture of all three colors, and some were a light blue. They climbed in and out of the opening of the wooden carrier track in the barn used to move the hay into the loft. They nested on ledges in the barn. During the summer, a pigeon nest had as many as four or five hatchings. When there was a large number they would fly up as a flock and make a big noise. Walter sometimes shot into the flock with his shotgun to thin them. The pigeons went to the feed bunks and picked up loose grain or corn around the hog pen.

The barn swallows returned every year and when they arrived it was a sign of the time for corn planting. The same pairs of swallows returned to the barn and the same nests year after year. Their arrival brought the joy of knowing it was time to plant corn.

Grandpa Bruner Lovaire Groff, who had raised Enid, died following her 30th birthday dinner. He was sitting in a rocking chair on the porch just after eating dinner when his head fell back in cardiac arrest. That morning he had washed his 1931 Model A Ford. In later years, Walter said that Grandpa Groff washed his car for his own funeral. Walter bought the car for $200. It had 12,000 miles on it and was the only family car until it was traded for a new 1939 Ford V-8 sedan bought with money Walter inherited from his Grandmother Happel.

Iowa summers were hot and humid. The worst drought year was 1934 and corn only made fifteen to twenty bushels to the acre. Oats and hay crops were nil in that drought. It was the year the road past Walter's farm was graded for graveling, but it was the next year before it was changed from mud to gravel. What a relief to have a better road for weekly marketing travel to the city. It was a sore point that Walter had to live with so many inconveniences when in his youth he had been accustomed to living in a modern farm home with indoor plumbing and electricity and a paved highway to the city, and now his oldest brother lived on the largest farm the family owned, 200 acres that had a new modern farmhouse with bathroom, steam heat, hot and cold running water and an improved road to U.S. 30 called the Lincoln Highway.

In 1934, Walter bought a new binder in partnership with his older brother. The cost of the binder was $350.00. It was sold in 1950 by a salesman for their Uncle August's Happel & Sons Implement Company, to a buyer for $100.00. That binder also cut father's younger brother's oats when he was having problems with his binder. All three Krug brothers cut oats together and were in threshing rings together: 1st cousin Marvin Happel's threshing machine for harvesting oats for three years; eight years in 1st cousin Billy Rammelsberg's threshing ring.

During the "Great Depression" years, men from Missouri in need of work came into Iowa to join threshing rings. Harvesting time was hard work and long days that meant they could be hired to shock oats and help with the threshing. When grain was heavy, a man could work for an hour and not see what he had done.

Bundles of oats wilted after they lay on the field for awhile. This wilting made oats shocking more difficult. The shocks held together when the oats was green, but as soon as the bundles wilted in the heat, the shocks had a tendency to fall apart. This was why farmers preferred to cut oats while the grain was still a little green. The goal was always to shock all the oats into bundles the same day it was cut.

The "Great Depression" hired men were given board and room for a week and $24.00 pay to divide between them on Saturday. The men would drive back to Missouri to spend Sunday with their family and be back to work in Iowa again on Monday morning. In 1950, Walter quit cutting oats with a tractor and binder, and eliminated threshing completely when he bought a motorized automatic harvester that cut the oats and gathered the grain all in one operation.

When Waler began farming he had three teams of horses, six to plow sod, plant and cultivate corn, make hay and harvest crops. Two of his horses were getting old and in not too long he had only four left, two teams, so he decided to breed one of his mares and raise a colt. When it was born it had lock jaw, a disease of the navel, and died immediately. The veterinary was unable to save it. The only comfort was when the breeder only charged one half of the $25.00 stud fee. It helped make the decision to change over to the machine age before the spring work began.

In the midst of a January 1936 blizzard, Walter's younger brother was married to a German farmer's daughter he met at a rural dance. The evening ceremony was held at the bride's rural farm home. It was freezing traveling the twenty-five miles to the wedding in a snowstorm blowing so hard Walter had to keep stopping the car to dig through snowdrifts with a scoop shovel that was carried in the car trunk. It took two hours to travel those twenty-five miles. The storm got worse in traveling west to the bride's farm home.

"We're not going to leave early to start for home once we get there. We'll stay all night, if we have to," Walter warned not wanting to miss any of the ceremony or reception festivities. The children fell asleep among the coats piled high in an upstairs bedroom while the wedding reception continued downstairs into the wee hours of the morning. Beer flowed freely and Walter's cousin played accordion music for singing and dancing in the farm house basement. There were candy bars and half filled glasses of beer passed to the children who congregated upstairs in the bedrooms to play and pass the hours.

The return trip to our farm home was difficult driving on ice and snow covered roads, but it was managed safely just before daybreak the following morning. It was an event long remembered for how cold it was inside the car, colder than it could ever be remember in winter travel due to determination to not miss the wedding even though the weather was not favorable.

Walter bought his first tractor in March 1936. He traded one horse and a "gang plow" for the Oliver 70 tractor, plow and disc. His Uncle August Happel, Happel & Sons Implement Co., allowed him $150.00 for the horse on the trade-in. The tractor cost $850.00, the two bottom plow $90.00, and disc $175.00. Walter borrowed $750.00 from the People's Bank in Cedar Rapids at 5% interest to make the deal. The president of the bank was a cousin who loaned the money requiring, only holding a life insurance policy as collateral. A year later, Walter purchased a two-row tractor cultivator. The tractor also took over the plowing of timothy sod from the horse drawn method in which occasionally the plow would not scour. With a tractor sod furrows were clean and neat and the furrow wall straight and smooth.

There were few conveniences in Walter and Enid's farm home built on a foundation of native stone with a steep pitched roof, one bedroom downstairs and four bedrooms on the second floor to be reached by a steep, narrow stairs. The house had ten foot ceilings on the first floor. The kitchen was the largest room in the house. Wainscotting, a third of the way up the walls, covered all four walls of the kitchen. A clock shelf, a wall magazine rack, built-in cupboard to the top of the ten foot ceiling, and several calendars that changed annually made up the simple décor of the rural farm home.

The kitchen table in the center of the room was the work surface area and center of family living. A kerosene lamp hanging from the center of the high ceiling was the only light in the room other than that which came through the windows of the door and the two windows on the west side of the room. All the other walls had doorways that led either into the dining room, downstairs bedroom, stairs to the cellar, and stairs to the second floor or doorway to the washroom off of the south wall.

A galvanized washtub served as a bath tub when it was brought into the kitchen and set in front of the cookstove with the oven door open to provide extra heat for bathers on Saturday night. Enid stoked the stove earlier in the evening to be sure there was hot water in the stove reservoir. There was only enough water for everyone in the family to bathe in the same water and mother decreed the order of baths. She liked to sponge the children first, but the water was too hot ofen and they begged to wait. Enid took the first bath, followed by the children. Walter bathed last because he was the dirtiest and the water was then not fit for anyone else's bathing use.

There were no conveniences on the farm in those years. The smallest house situated inconspicuously behind the wood shed in the backyard, by the vineyard, was the outside privy or "shindilly" as it was called. It was used all seasons of the year. It was cold sitting there in winter. It was necessary to brush snow that had sifted inside it before sitting down in winter, and spiders and webs needed to be brushed away in the summer months. The farm was one of Iowa's unimproved farms that lacked indoor plumbing. Sears Roebuck and Montgomery Ward catalogues furnished the toilet paper. The slickness of the paper was not pleasant, but the alternative was corn cobs and that was even worse to use.

"Did you fall in?" The inevitable words said when someone stayed too long and kept the door locked so nobody else could enter. That was sometimes a problem all seasons of the year.

Popcorn was raised in large quantities in the family vegetable garden, located distant enough from the field corn, to prevent cross pollination. Snacking was a great pastime of families, especially during the winter months when there was a hot fire going in the kitchen cook stove. Popping corn, making taffy or homemade fudge, and home churning of ice-cream were the evening activities of sitting around in the kitchen to keep warm.

Children had burns on their hands caused by feeding corncobs in the front and side door of the cook stove to stoke the fire, a job assigned to keep the fire hot enough to heat the oven for baking and cooking meals. In summer, peaches were bought in a light weight wooden bushel basket and that basket became the container for corn cobs making it easier for children to carry a bushel of corncobs into the house. Corncobs made fast hot fires, but it was necessary to keep feeding them into the stove because they burned up rapidly. A hazard of the thin wooden peach baskets was slivers that ran into hands and under fingernails when continuously scooping up the short corncobs to feed the fire. When Enid discovered the cause of frequent slivers, the peach basket was replaced with a metal bushel basket that was heavier and more difficult to carry.

Another chore was helping carry wood every day to fill the wood box behind the corncob basket beside the cook stove. Every evening before dark the wood box needed to be filled.

Also, it ws necessary to fill the reservoir on the end of the cook stove with water. A full pail of water was too heavy, and more trips were necessary to fill it instead of putting so much water in the pail.

When Walter completed chores to come in for the evening meal, the tin sound of the pails he carried hitting sides clanged as he set them down on the porch to take off his eight-buckle overshoes. Then closing of the kitchen door signaled that supper was near at hand. Walter had to wash two and three times in the washroom, located just off the kitchen, to remove the soil and dirt from farming before he could sit down to eat a meal.

F.D.R.'s promise in the White House that all farmers would have rural electrification came true in July and August 1936 when Henry Krug extended the electric power line from the neighbors, a quarter a mile away, to our farm and we had electricity for the first time. Walter and Enid drove to Cedar Rapids and purchased an electric Crosley refrigerator for $218 from Walter's first cousin, owner of Standard Appliance Company, who always gave a discount when Walter made a purchase. The deal included a free Sunbeam "mixmaster" for Enid. The refrigerator sat in the corner of the kitchen for some months before electric wiring was completed on the farm so that the refrigerator could be turned on and used.

There had always been electricity at the railroad roundhouse and bunkhouse of the Milwaukee Railroad located across a field, a distance of about fifty rods, from Walter's road gate. The railroad was responsible for the origin of our rural town, a mile from our farm. A railroad section foreman gave the town its name. Ten rows of switch tracks long enough to hold eighty to ninety freight train cars made it possible to back up freight trains and engines to wait for servicing at the roundhouse or to sidetrack trains needing sudden repair or if trains needed to pass on the main tracks.

"What's going on at the railroad?" was the inevitable question when noise pierced the air, hurting ears and jarring the windows of the farm house.

"The roundhouse is full again," Walter answered. "The ten switch tracks are full too." The roundhouse operated twenty-four hours a day, seven days a week. Noise pollution from the sixteen to eighteen stalls filled to capacity was at times unbearable to young ears. Additionally, there were as many as three or four switch engines that pushed trains around at all times. Engines were placed on the roundhouse turntable and revved up at full steam speed while standing still, producing a powerful shaking vibration which shook the farmhouse windows.

"If I could have been what I wanted to be, I would have been a railroad engineer." Walter's younger brother said in table mealtime conversations at Walter and Enid's farm home. He could not resist the fascination of the "iron horse," as he called it when he watched the close railroad.

Besides the roundhouse, bunkhouse, and restaurant, an icehouse and a coal tipple made from huge wooden beams were located across from our farm. Walter climbed to the top of the coal tipple several times and enjoyed recalling the view from that vantage point. When Diesel locomotives began to be used the 103 foot high coal tipple became obsolete. The tipple, a coal-loading structure, was the last remaining facility of a million-dollar installation built by the Milwaukee Railroad at Atkins in 1917 to be torn down when the railroad center was completely removed in the later part of the 20th century.

The railroad icehouse was filled with large square blocks of ice brought by train from the eastern states Great Lakes in the winter months to store them covered with sawdust that kept them frozen through the summer months.

A special treat for July 4th holiday or during a mild winter when ice was not available, Walter walked across the narrow field between our road gate and the railroad carrying a gunny sack, an ice pick, and a hammer. In the ice-house he chipped off a chuck of ice large enough, but not too large, to carry home and churn a freezer full of homemade ice-cream. It could hardly seem possible ice would not melt in the ice-house during the hot days of Iowa summer. The huge cavern filled with ice covered in sawdust was enough to last all year.

The Union Pacific streamliners from Grand Central Station in Chicago passed Walter and Enid's farm about an hour apart each afternoon headed west. If they left Chicago on time, they were still on time traveling at one-hundred miles an hour. Walter watched daily for the east bound streamliners by the same name to notice if they were late coming in from the west.

"My watch needs repairing," Walter complained when he often noticed his pocket watch and the streamliner's arrival time did not jibe. The fine siftings of soil, especially in spring and summer farm work, often played havoc with a pocket watch in his overalls. When eastbound streamliners failed to pass through our area, he made a point of listening to the 10'clock evening news on the radio to find out if there had been inclement weather in the west or a train wreck. If he heard nothing on the radio, he talked with the railroad teletype agent in our rural town to find out if there had been a derailment.

Noise from the railroad was so great in Walter and Enid's farm home that at times they suffered from it. It was necessary to yell at each other to be heard above the steam engine noise and necessary to stand right beside each other to be heard or so words could be understood.

Another loud noise on the farm was the shrill noise of the Katydid, a seven year cyclic locust that looked like a huge grasshopper. In the most intense heat of summer, some years as early as the middle of July, but usually in August and September, the piercing noise of the Katydid could be heard daily. Katydids perched on the lowest limb of the Ash tree in either the front yard or the back yard of the house. It was an uncomfortable wing rubbing noise that hurt human ears.

"If you see anyone walking into our road gate and they are not your relatives, run and get me right away. Do not talk to them!" Walter and Enid warned about strangers walking on the gravel road between the railroad and our farm. "Beggars" rode the railroad cars and got off at the roundhouse looking for food. The roundhouse did not give free meals away and the "beggars" started walking to the nearest road and our farm house was the first place where they stopped.

"Some people haven't food. We've food because we're not lazy and grow our own. Those who're hungry and willing to work, we'll not turn away," Walter said.

Sometimes Enid saw strangers walking into the farm yard. She went to the house and watched to see the stranger approach. If she thought Walter would approve of the man, she sent the "beggar" to the field to find Walter and get an assignment of farm work. If Walter approved of the man, he brought the "beggar" to the house and talked with Enid, and made arrangements for a specific amount of labor to be accomplished on the farm. Usually, it was cutting and stacking wood for the furnace winter fuel supply.

The "good beggars," willing to work for a meal, kept the wood supply cut, stacked and ready for winter. If Walter approved of the finished work, Enid prepared a meal and served it to the "beggar" on the back porch. In that way, it was possible to share the bounty of their harvest with the less fortunate deemed deserving of it.

Communication is the lifeblood of extended family relationships. The American Dream, a term coined in the Great Depression to describe the national ideal of an open society with equal opportunity, meant shared sacrifice and shared reward in the Krug extended farming business. Henry Krug, his sons, and their families, pooled their labor with a strong, prideful determination to accomplish all the tasks of farming many acres of land.

"Germans are alright if you really work," Enid said, "and if you have a sense of humor." She thought her German in-laws were "very direct." She also discovered outstanding characteristics in Germans in their dependability and precision.

Confronted by the tough reality of an extended family farming operation, Walter and his three brothers wanted more than anything to strike out on their own in farming. In-laws wished to be independent of the extended farming business as a way to gain more control over their lives.

"It's going to be harder," Walter said when extended family problems arose. "You can work day in and day out and there's not much you can do about it," he reminded.

Enid's gold rimmed china dishes, a set of twelve place settings, she bought with her teacher earnings just before she was married, gradually dwindled in numbers of plates, cups and saucers as they were her only dishes and she used them everyday. When a full table was set for harvesters she used what was left of Christina Krug's best set of dishes that she purchased at Henry Krug's retirement auction sale.

Walter smoked cigars whenever he relaxed long enough to just sit in the house or when he was visiting with relatives. His father, Henry Krug, started smoking cigarettes when he lived with Walter and Enid working on the farm that he owned. Walter warned that his father was going to get into trouble if he kept on smoking cigarettes.

"Look! Look! Enid yelled while running into the kitchen. She was laughing so hard it was not possible to figure out what was going on. Her father-in-law Henry Krug was lighting up a cigarette in the dining room, and a cool breeze going through the open windows started his mustache on fire. The motions he went through in putting out the fire were amusing. The next time they saw their Krug parent he had shaved off his mustache. They never forgot when their father-in-law's mustache burned.

Henry Krug was dedicated to the soil. He was devoted to farming even though he spent a lot of time in carpentry. His four sons married and settled on his four farms. He had seventeen grandchildren. Henry Krug wanted nothing as much as his children and grandchildren's well-being.

Working days were long when Walter's father, Henry, lived on the farm with them. He was there to improve the buildings and worked long hours, from early dawn to the darkness of night. Meals were the only time the family gathered together. It was then Henry answered Enid's questions about his German grandparents and their Old World home in Europe. Those conversations were remembered as pleasant combinations of German and English language. Walter and and his father conversed in German about it. Enid and her father-in-law talked genealogy in English.

Father-in-law Henry kept reminding Enid that the Michel family line in Iowa, who the Henry Krug's were related to, stemmed from Meta Michel. It was important to remember that because Michel men had the same name in more than one generation, only the wives names were different. He wanted to be sure Walter and Enid never became confused which branch of the Michel family tree was directly in their genealogy. It was easy to never forgotten the Meta Michel name because no one else ever had that first name.

The only thing father-in-law Henry Krug did that was displeasing was when he emptied the large galvanized washtub full of water that Enid filled and set in the sun to warm the water for children's play during the hottest days of summer. It was a way of helping children cool off. Grandpa Henry thought it a waste of water. He could not stand to see something undone around the farm yard and constantly monitored what needed to be done. As long as children played in the tub filled with water Grandpa Henry was no where to be seen. When everyone was away from the yard and the tub, Grandpa would empty it and turn it upside down to dry. Walter fussed about the expense of pumping water and the wasting of it by the children.

"We will be happy," Walter said. "We always have hope." Then he chuckled and all was well in the household.

"There's not an idle bone in your grandfather's body," my mother summed it up. Grandpa helped with the field work. He built a new chicken house; a new machine shed and tore down the old corn crib that was built in 1912. He hired a carpenter crew, made up of relatives, to build a large new corn crib with indoor elevator and large second floor storage bins for grain that cost $300 in 1940. We heard him pounding, straightening nails and sorting them at night by a light in the new corn crib. For all the problems that erupted from day to day, a grandparent's watchful eye provided a fundamental stability and sense of well-being in the family. Walter and Enid were "tight" with money, but their children possessed the richness of growing up equipped with experiences to deal with problems, an inheritance better than money in the bank.

It was during this same time that Henry Krug was living with his son and daughter-in-law that he began dressing up early in the evening and leaving the farm in his car. Enid did not know what he was doing until one day Walter told her he had been speaking with his father in the German language, and that his father was driving to Atkins to visit a German widow. He was courting her for a possible marriage, but she would have none of it. When Henry left the farm Walter and Enid lived on he bought a house on the main street of Atkins and lived there for quite a few years.

"The neighbor's cows broke into the back forty again," the upset in Walter's voice rang out. The fence must be fixed before they bloat up and die."

Enid ran to the wall telephone and cranked out two long rings and a short ring. When the neighbors, Walter's cousins, did not answer, Enid cranked frantically again, believing in her haste she had not clearly differentiated between long and short rings. Enid shouted into the phone, hoping someone would hear her. There were eight families on our "party" line, each household had its own combination of long and short rings. Sometimes it was difficult to hear the difference between the long and the short cranked rings.

Walter ran to the barnyard to get the wire stretcher. It was possible to hear the tractor start and see him head for the back forty acres. Enid waved at Walter. It was another day in which he would be very busy. Iowa corn farmers had too much work to do.

The only time Walter's children saw him was when he gave directions about chores. He described the gates he had opened earlier in the day that must close before the cattle were driven from the field to the watering tank. Seven gates surrounded the barnyard. The gates were made of rows of barbed wire, several were heavy wooden structures; one was made of iron and wire. Three or more gates often had to be closed before heading for the field to round up the cattle. On harvest days all seven gates were opened and all had to be closed before walking in the farm lane to the fields to herd the cattle to the farm yard.

Going after cattle was pleasant in that it gave the opportunity to view most of the farm along the way. Walter and Enid's roots were deep in the fertile soil of the Midwestern prairie. The American Dream as persistent and powerful in an extended farming family as when the earliest ancestors came from the European Old World. With hard work, frugal habits and the grace of God, the land produced more than enough to support a family. How much more was Walter's secret.

CHAPTER 7
The Changing Seasons

Sunday was the only day of the week when the Krug men relaxed from the hard work of seasonal farming. Walter, his father Henry Krug, Great Uncles George and William Krug, still dressed in their best worsted business suits from attending church in the morning, pushed away from the dining room table after saying a prayer of Thanksgiving in German for each having consumed two plates full of beef, mashed potatoes and gray, buttered corn, green beans, gelatin salad, fresh baked yeast rolls, and a third plate full of desserts: open-faced apple pie topped with freshly whipped cream, home grown and canned peaches, oatmeal cookies and frosted nut cake.

"The food in this country is better than in Germany," the men expressed when they spoke in English, "We don't eat Weiner Schnitzel here!"

Before the meal they prayed: "Gewaehre uns deine Gnade, O Gott, dass, ob wir essen oder trinken, oder was immer wir tun, wir moegen alles in deinem Namen und zu deiner ehre tun. Amen." (Grant us Thy Grace, O Lord that whether we eat or drink, or whatsoever we do, we may do it all in Thy name and to Thy Glory. Amen.)

The dining room wall had a framed plaque in the English language:
> Christ is the head of this house.
> The unseen guest at ever meal.
> The silent listener to every conversation.

Invitations for Sunday dinner were often made at the last minute, following church service, when worshipers gathered in front of the church to visit before returning to their cars.

That is when Walter invited his German brothers, or uncles and families to our home for a meal when there were no other activites planned. Enid did not always go to church. In winter months she suffered from "sinus trouble" and preferred to sit by the furnace register and read seed catalogs to plan her summer flower and vegetable garden.

After eating dinner the men in the family retired to the living room to continue talking in the German language while the women washed and dried the dishes.

The men played horseshoes under the trees on Walter's farm when there were family gatherings for Sunday dinners or reunions. Walter put a horseshoe over the roots of a tree east of the hog house. The tree grew so fast that by that summer he had to chop it out just below the ground so he just left the horseshoe there. Usually the stakes for the game were set in the ground thirty-five feet apart.

"The men in the Krug family are the most mannerly and kind men you will ever meet," Enid told her children. They never left the house after having eaten a meal without going to her to shake her hand and thank her for the food and the invitation to the meal.

The Krug parents, Henry and Christina, were both raised in families of ten children. There were many aunts and uncles to visit on weekend evenings in winter months and to meet at family reunions in the summer. Enid kept a record of those who invited us to their home for dinner so she could reciprocate. It was a busy social life and a time to catch up on what was going on in farming in the large extended family.

Every day, all four seasons of the year, Enid started breakfast with oatmeal, a part of her Scottish traditional way of life. She made toast over hot coals in the cook stove until she had electricity and an electric toaster. There was always plenty of butter and milk from Walter's weekly trips to the Cedar Valley Creamery to market the sweet cream he sold for Grade A butterfat from his Holstein milking herd. Another carryover from Enid's youth seemed like a peculiar habit to

Walter, the dipping of her table napkin into her water glass when she dined in restaurants. It embarrassed Walter who could not come to terms with the fact that Enid had been raised with finger bowls at the table in the home of her Scottish Grandmother "Nettie."

Haymaking in June was the end of spring and it launched summer on the farm. Time was important. There were never enough hours in a summer day to get the hay raked and mowed before the threat of a summer storm, and then there were never enough hours to get all the cut hay into the barn before another summer storm threatened. It was truly important to "make hay while the sun shines."

Walter sometimes used a hay fork called a "needle" which looked like a huge darning needle with a rope threaded through the eye of the steel loading device. A long slim needle, it did not take a large load of loose hay off the wagon and many needle setting were required to empty a very full hayrack. At other times, a big grapple fork was used that was shaped like an inverted U. After the fork had been shoved down in the hay, spurs snapped out at a ninety degree angle on the end of tines and kept the hay from sliding off. When the fork was full of hay it was lifted by a long rope on a pulley at the top of the barn that was pulled by a team of horses. When the load reached the top of the barn, the fork rolled inside the loft on a track that hung from the ceiling of the haymow. By jerking a rope the spurs retracted and the hay on the fork dropped in a chosen location in the haymow.

Walter's brother, who lived on the next farm, set the hayfork in unloading the hayrack at Walter's barn so he could arrange the hay in the barn, the dirtiest job of haymaking. Everything went smoothly until the hayfork started up from the hayrack wagon and the trip rope got wrapped around the brother's ankle. Just before the fork full of hay reached the top of the barn to roll inside the loft, the rope became so tight it dumped all the hay on top of father's brother.

September rains splashed tree leaves, beating them to the ground and autumn grew increasingly cold. Rivulets of rain poured down on the stalks of milkweed along the roadside ditch. The dashing of water through the gravel road culverts could also be heard. The wind and rain and the land met; one force moving, the other resisting. Not a battle with winning and losing, but simply natural change made swift enough that everyone could realize what was happening.

Farmers watched the climate to determine work schedules. It was not uncommon for the sky to grow dark and heavy. September was a month of heavy rainfall on the Great Plains of Iowa. Sometimes the sky looked as if the sun had set, although it was not yet 4:00 p.m.

A cold, chilling Artic wind blew out of the northwest across the prairie. Flakes of snow mingled with rain and froze on the windows that even had storm windows covering them. The frost level on Iowa farms varied from one foot to four feet depending upon the severity of winter weather. "It doesn't go five feet deep," Walter said. Some years the heavy snow and frost was continuous until after the snow melted to bare ground in spring months. The frost level went down deeper every day when there was bare ground and extremely cold weather. When there was snow coverage on the ground, the frost level did not penetrate as deeply into the soil. Underground it might not be more than 8-10 inches.

The frost level made a difference in building fences in spring and fall, the time of the year when there was time for such tasks. There were four foot deep end posts and it was necessary to replace corner posts or put them in when there was no frost. When there was no frost—spring, summer, fall—post holes were dug into ground two and one-half to three feet deep. Some winters the frost was one and one-half feet deep.

Walter had a milking herd of twelve Holstein cows. One year he had cows on the other side of the barn in addition to those in the twelve milking stanchions. Fresh cows gave more milk than those that had been milked for awhile. The milk was separated and the cream was sold for Grade A butterfat. The price varied from fifteen cents a pound for butterfat to a high of sixty cents a pound. The cream was cooled in cream cans in a cold water tank in the house basement. The ten gallon cans weighed approximately twenty-eight to thirty pounds empty and 110 to 112 pounds when full. The five gallon cans weighed fifteen to sixteen pounds empty and fifty-six to fifty-seven pounds when full. The heavy heft of the cans was from galvanized tin. Some creameries retined the cans as they became older to eliminate any rust.

A De Laval milking machine was installed in the barn and Walter no longer allowed anyone to milk the cows by hand. He did not want dirt to get into the milk from the hands or from touching teats. I milked the cows with the machine for a week at a time several years when I was in high school because my father was in bed those years after he finished planting the corn on the 15th of May. His knees were so sore that he could not walk. Dr. Bradley was called to the house and ordered him to rest in bed for a week each time. I was up at daybreak each morning, brought the cows into the barn stanchions, fed and milked them, and cleaned the manure out of the milking barn.

Enid helped me push the heavy pails filled with milk in a little red wagon to the cream separator. She separated the milk and helped me carry the milk to feed it to the hogs. Then it was time to feed the horses and lead them to the water tank each morning and evening. It was fun to look for the fish that were put in the cattle water tank, bullheads that lived off the grain that fell out of the mouths of cattle and horses when they drank water. There were gates to open and close for the cattle before I could go to the house and get ready to ride the school bus to high school each morning.

Many early spring and summer mornings began with the announcement by a rooster: "Cock-a-doodle-do!" Crowing roosters and the chirping of sparrows around the hog pens were usual sounds that all is well on the farm. Children were expected to pitch in instead of being given an allowance. There was no sitting for hours watching television or listening to the radio.

There were few things to play with so we honed our imaginations by competing to see who could conjure the most images in clouds drifting overhead in the azure blue sky of the Great Plains prairie. More often than not I won, earning a reputation as someone with an eye for aesthetic detail. It seemed to be a natural sense I had besides being a hard worker, both native elements fostered by my combined German and Scotch culture.

In spring, when crop planting was nearly finished, or at least the end was in sight, our family joined an uncle and his family after church on Sunday to drive nineteen miles south of our farm to Amana to eat dinner at the Colony Inn. The restaurant was formerly the community kitchen of the Amana colony, one of seven religious colonies that opened in 1932 to the public for serving family style meals. It was the only restaurant where we ate a meal for many years and operated by German people from the state of Hessen, in Germany, the same state of the Krug family in Europe.

The people of the Amana Colonies fled their German homeland in 1842 to practice their religion without interference from the state which controlled both religion and government in Germany. In 1932, feeling the pressures of the capitalistic culture in the United States, the Amanas abandoned a system of pure communal living for a market economy. The share-and-share a like system run by church elders who controlled both the spiritual and financial sectors of the Amana society was swapped for a separation of church and state. The Amanas call that switch the "Great Change."

The Colony Inn restaurant was very popular on Sunday because of the delicious food they served inexpensively. Large crowds gathered on the lawn outside the restaurant to wait in line until their number came up for a table. Walter and his brother walked into the restaurant upon arrival, while the women and children of our family gathered with the crowd waiting on the lawn, and they spoke for a table directly to the owner of the restaurant in both his and their native German dialect. It was only a matter of minutes before the restaurant owner appeared on the porch and called out, "Krug brothers!" We were given the first reset table that was ready and would accommodate our family size. It was a time when we were given special treatment because of our German heritage.

First memories of eating at the Colony Inn cost fifty cents for children's meals. Adults paid one dollar for every choice of meat, except steak which cost $1.50 for the whole meal. Orders were taken for choice of meat only. Each person was served an individual platter of meat of choice: pork sausage, ham, chicken, or steak. Every table had large bowls served family style of mashed potatoes, gravy, dressing, cottage cheese, applesauce, cold slaw salad, northern beans, sauerkraut, corn or peas, Amana baked white and whole wheat bread. The bowls were filled as soon as they began to look empty.

It was an "all you can eat" menu and the men in our family dished up more than once and loved that place to eat. Dessert was a choice of pie—apple, peach, coconut-cream, cherry, pumpkin, two crust rhubarb (in season), most served à la mode. It was all served on blue and white damask table cloths in a simple rural dining hall atmosphere. The furnishings and menu remained the same over all the years. It was one of the events the whole family looked forward to when it was decided, on a moment's notice, to drive to the Amanas to eat. The men thought meals at the Colony Inn were like threshing meals without the work for women in the family that went with harvesting.

There was not beautiful weather to start all summer days. Some were dull, gray days. Big heavy clouds came in low. When they opened up, rain came down in sheets. It was a cold rain. The thought of going out into the weather to move cattle from one pasture to another was dreadful. The cattle had to be driven a half mile against a strong, steady wind that whipped the rain into pellets that stung like buckshot.

The cattle were sluggish. They crowded up against the fence with their tails to the wind, their heads down. When they finally started to walk, they twisted their necks to keep from getting hit full in the face by the wind and rain. In their wake, they left a mushy trail of mud. The family dog worked back and forth barking behind the cattle like a pendulum at the rear of the herd.

In summer vacations from school, children in the family herded cattle in the ditches along the gravel road past our farm. Walter locked the cattle in the barnyard after milking in the morning. Then he hollered up the stairway for children to get up out of bed and herd the cattle until the noon whistle blew in Atkins, a mile away which we could easily hear. Herding the cattle along the ditches extended the pasture in summer and kept the ditch grass and weeds down at the same time. Enid used a needle to dig the tiny red chiggers out of the bites around the children's waist, arms and legs from sitting in the tall grass in the ditches watching the cattle. The morning hours seemed very long when herding cattle.

Enid got up at daybreak to go to the garden and pick vegetables, and always had work lined up in summer for children to gather, core and cut up apples for piemaking, potatoes to peel and soak in a pan of cold water, peas to shell, tomatoes to wash and peel. She hoed the weeds in the garden before the heat of the day.

It was the children's job to pick the stickery gooseberries in the fence rows by the orchard and the raspberries in a dense patch had to be climbed through to pick the ripe berries. Cherries, plums, and peaches all had their season for children to gather them as they ripened. There were wild elderberries to pick in the road ditches along the farm. Children were always busy picking or shelling something for meals or canning when not doing anything else.

The trees in the orchard were all producing when Walter and Enid moved to the farm. Apple varities include: Snow Apple, Roman Stem, Greenings, Yellow Transparent, Wolf River (very large apple), Wealthy, Red Delicious, Golden Delicious, Jonathan, Dutchess (early cooking apple, not as good eaten raw). The Greenings tree, a winter apple was picked in early October just before a heavy frost. A light frost helped ripen the Greenings' apples, the tree produced as many as fourteen bushels of apples a season and they were stored in cool temperatures and used throughout the winter.

Some early summer Sunday mornings it was possible to hear parents talking at the breakfast table downstairs loud enough and hear that they were arguing about whether or not to go away from home that day. If the weather was threatening in any way, Walter would not speak kindly about leaving home. He did not like driving around on sloppy roads that only made his car dirty. Hearing the tone in his voice decided if Enid was making any headway with her plans to travel that day. When successful, she prepared picnic food including sandwiches and a can of pork-and-beans. Without canned beans there was never enough food to satisfy Walter. She included children's books and games, if it was a long drive, the camera, and the "rag". Before we left home, she always wet an old washcloth and put it into a plastic bread sack. She perspicaciously handed it out to wipe sticky fingers and faces, or to clean up spills.

Enid liked to pack the car on summer Sundays and head for the nearest state park. She thought Walter's discontent from hard work from time to time was the need to be more outgoing with more interests. Early on Sunday morning Enid cooked eggs for deviling them, made potato salad, picked tomatoes and often had great difficulty talking father into missing church to travel for the day. If a region of the state suffered climatic misfortune from hail or flood, Walter was more interested in driving there to look at the crops. It always made him feel more fortunate and twice blessed when he returned home to look at his own fields.

"There's nothing to see there..." Walter whined when Enid tried to motivate him to pack a picnic lunch and drive to a certain state park.

"Just a couple of Indian trails..." Walter insisted even though Enid disagreed. True, many Iowa State Parks preserved Indian mounds, caves and waterfalls abounding in Indian legends.

There was argument over whether to drive a distance to a state park and picnic there or along the way. In August, after all the harvesting was completed, Walter honored Enid's desire to travel by taking her to Illinois to a reunion of her Scottish relatives.

Several years there were three week vacations in August to drive to Salt Lake City to visit Grandpa Bryner. Along the way there was time to enjoy the Badlands of South Dakota, the Black Hills with its amazing Mt. Rushmore, and Yellowstone National Park in Wyoming. After two weeks, Walter started talking about going home and his conversations never left out the farm. He was almost miserable until he could return home and tell all that he had seen to his younger brother who was also his lifelong closest friend.

In later years, Walter and Enid went fishing in Minnesota for a week during college summer vacations and I did all the farm chores for them for a week at a time. The chores included canning home-grown peaches that were ripe at that time besides all the daily farm chores. It was very exhausting causing me to never want to live on a farm in future years.

Walter had eighty breeding sows a year. With eight to ten sows he would get about one hundred pigs, but usually only had six or eight to a sow so could not get a ten average. Hogs will never overeat. In six months from birth they usually went to the market. As time went on hogs went to the market in five months making a second paycheck from the milk and corn they ate. In later years, he bought feeder pigs, as many as

140 at a time and made more money buying feeder pigs than from raising his own pigs.

Cholera struck the hogs twice. One year the hogs were not vaccinated for it when the disease struck. The other time a bunch of feeder pigs were supposed to have been vaccinated when purchased. Quite a few died when Cholera broke out in them. They were then vaccinated immediately. It cost fifty cents to one dollar and fifty cents a hog to vaccinate them, depending upon the size of the hog. The white hogs raised were Berkshires. He also had Hampshires and spotted ones. He bought some hogs in Missouri that were vaccinated.

A cob and wood stove was used to heat water for laundry in a wood shed alongside our family farm house. A wash boiler was used to heat the water. One Monday morning in the last of August, when Walter was loading loose straw by the cow yard, he saw smoke coming out of the doors and windows of the wood house. He does not remember what he did with the wagon and team of horses, but he jumped off the wagon and ran to the building. Later, he found his pitchfork in the garden. He ran to the cistern along the east side of the house and pumped buckets of water and threw them on the building. It just made a little steam. He crawled on his hands and knees and tried to pull the washing machine out of the building, but the machine had a gasoline engine with exhaust out of the window, and it stuck so tight he had to crawl back out so he would not be overcome by fire and smoke. The intense heat singed his eyelashes and eyebrows.

Enid phoned the central telephone operator for the Atkins Fire Department and the operator rang the fire whistle from the switch board and the volunteer firemen ran quickly to the fire truck and came immediately and sprayed water on the side of the house next to the building. The white paint on the house blistered from the high heat of the fire. Grandpa Henry Krug paid the fire department for their services.

Everything in the building was lost to the fire including the washing machine and cream separator which were both new:

shotgun, bullets, tools, new school clothing, a new bicycle, wash tubs, can of gas for the washing machine, sheepskin-lined duck coat which was never replaceable, and fuel for kindling the furnace and house cook stove. Grandpa Henry Krug owned the farm and had insurance on the buildings. He was given a good settlement on the building and all its contents. He built a new replacement building and also a new outdoor toilet located next to the building that had also burned in the fire. The major fire loss was personal property and school clothes that could not be exactly replaced including the bicycle.

The soot in the house brick chimney from the furnace in the basement to the roof caught on fire one winter night. The fire shooting out of the top of the chimney was noticed as far away as Atkins and the fire department phoned to inquire if our house was on fire. Walter shoveled the fire out of the furnace using a large handle shovel so it would not gas the house. The chimney got so hot from the soot fire in it that it scorched the paint on the plastered surface of the chimney in the dining room and on an upstairs bedroom. The next day there were black ashes all over the snow in the yard around the house.

When Grandpa Henry Krug and his sons ate meals at Walter and Enid's home the subject of the Milwaukee Railroad came up in talk around the table because it was just across the road from the farm. The closest railroad building was a bunkhouse that accommodated fifty to sixty men. At one time there were two restaurants built there. Later, there was only one restaurant and Walter ate there a lot in his last years on the farm in the 1960's. When Enid was away at her meetings or when his longtime school friend, Leslie Lensch, visited the two of them went to the railroad restaurant to eat since it was only a short walk across the roadgate and a narrow field. In summer months, the distance was so close it was often possible to hear the railroad men talking at the bunkhouse.

In the late 1940's diesel engines began to pull the trains on the ten switch tracks across from the farm. Then the latest coal burning steam engines that were almost new were taken off the freight trains. It was possible to see five and six diesel engines pulling one and a half mile trains. Usually there were three or four diesel engines pulling one train.

Walter saw many World War II troop trains heading East before the invasion of Europe in June 1944. There were so many troop trains heading east that all the sidetracks across from his farm were full waiting to go on East at the right time. Big old freight engines pounded through the Atkins railroad tracks pulling the troop trains. Troop trains were unscheduled. The engines were called "Big Boys" and "Mountain Mallees" that had two sets of drive wheels and two sets of cylinders.

When the full steam turntable at the roundhouse was running in the middle of the night, the loud noise caused anyone asleep to immediately sit up straight in bed. Walter got out of bed and went to each room to tell everyone to go back to sleep, that it was only the railroad making that noise. He said the roundhouse began dying down in the late 1930's. There used to be four big boilers that burned coal to make steam and heat, but there were never more than three in operation at a time, one was always under repair.

Tramps, called "bums," rode in railroad freight cars and got off at the Atkins railroad center, walked the short distance across a field and across the gravel road to the closest farm. When they arrived, Enid met them at the house steps and sent them to find Walter. He took them to the woodlot and promised them a meal if they chopped wood for several hours that could be burned in our furnace; however, they refused to work for a meal. The number of "bums" who came to the farm over time made it apparent there must have been a method of marking the farm as a place where it was easy to get a meal.

At least once every summer our family drove across the Mississippi River to a reunion of Enid's Scottish[1] Illinois relatives. The toll bridge across the river at Clinton, Iowa, was twenty cents per car for many years. At Savannah, Illinois, the toll bridge cost thirty-five to forty-five cents. The Davenport, Iowa, Interstate 80 bridge across the Mississippi River was free and that was the best place to cross the big river.

One beautiful September day a wedding reception was held at the next door neighbors, Walter's Happel relatives, when their daughter was married. It was a traditional German marriage celebration. Many tables were set up on their large farm house yard lawn and the evening meal was served outdoors. It was a beautiful day for the early evening reception. The children saved their squares of thick white icing, silver décor centering each frosting cluster, from the wedding cake and kept it dried for years as a souvenir. The children enjoyed peeking around every corner to see the bride as much as possible.

When darkness set in, the children gathered in the upstairs bedrooms to play games and entertain themselves. The men brought half filled glasses of beer up to the children as the evening progressed, and adults gathered in the basement to dance to a relative's accordion band. There was singing of "Ach, Du Lieber Augustein" and "Du, Du, Liegst Mir Im Herzen." Sometimes the children joined in the interesting sound of the syllables and sang though they did not know what the words meant.

The wedding reception lasted until midnight when the chivariers, an organized playful disturbance, arrived and made as much noise as possible so the groom would pay them off to leave. The groom's car was hidden some place other than either his parents or the bride's parents home to keep it from chivariers who would have their own way of marking it and possibly causing it to not start when it was time for the newly married couple to depart for their honeymoon. When the new church was completed in Atkins in 1941, it ended German home wedding celebrations; instead, church basement tea table or meal type receptions emerged.

When a breeze rustled all morning in the trees, bringing down leaves, it authenticated the arrival of autumn. It had been coming closer with every earlier sunset, every later dawn, with asters blooming and snowberries showing up. The shrubs along the gravel road ditches burst out in some bright red leaves.

Spiders strung their webs all through the garden, and walkway concentrating on the front steps, which had a fine filtering of air that encourages bugs to float along the line of least resistance. It was not just the spiders that do a lot of hunting in the sunny place. The chickadees, higher in the trees, constantly prowl through the branches, called *dee-dee-dee* to each other. Anyone going up or down the steps to the farmyard driveway would be announced by one or another bird call, or hear the whistle of dove's wings as they fly away, or the *clap-clap-clap* as pigeons take flight.

Wasps circled around the tips of the ash trees' branches. What did they find so attractive? A few weeks earlier the kadydids sat on these same branches. Occasionally, the shell of a kadydid that was discarded fell to the ground having emerged from many years of cyclic growth.

The leaves were also ready to fall because of the long dry summer and the sudden drop in temperature that came with the first heavy rains of autumn. That set of circumstances sent some of the plants in the farm garden into their change of color earlier than usual. In a week, the ash trees turned from green to gold and dropped every leaf.

It was an early autumn morning and the house felt chilly. The fire in the cook stove went out from Walter and Enid's early morning breakfast cooking as there was need to do outdoor morning chores. In checking the clock there was only a half-hour remaining before the start of school.

The teacher was always trying to make students think by asking difficult questions such as: "Will you be alive in the year 2000?" Then the teacher waited to see how many students held up their hands. From the earliest time and understanding of the meaning of that question, each time it was asked, students looked forward to being a witness to a milestone of the ages—the millennium.

The millennial concept has been around since the Book of Daniel in the Bible was written. Daniel in the Old Testament and Revelation chapter in the New Testament picture apocalyptic events associated with 1,000 year milestones. Students reconciled to the fact that the year 2000 would not just be a date on the calendar. There have been unparalleled progress on many fronts in humanity's search for its destiny—progress marred by greed, jealousy and all the other human failings—but progress nonetheless.

The "Great Depression" was always with the German and Scottish immigrants to Iowa. It left an indelible mark on them that surfaced at any moment in time. It was impossible for them to forget the change in cost as well as in the prices they received for their farm products.

Enid inherited a steel-strong survival kit of Scottish genes, and resilience, coupled with realism, physical courage, deeply felt principles and an unerring eye for the phony. True to Scottish culture and thrift, oatmeal was her favorite food to cook. She made it for the whole family every day. Oatmeal, sometimes hot but often already cold in the pan, waited for children for breakfast every morning. Parents ate a portion of it earlier in the morning and it was waiting when children finished dressing each morning. With plenty of sugar it was tolerable whether hot or cold.

Enid devoted all the cooking years of her life to making her Scottish style of oatcakes to stock the cookie jar. They were an oatmeal drop cookie often filled with raisins and sometimes with nuts, or whatever was on hand at the time of baking. She made so many of the thick oatmeal lumps that they became hard in the cookie jar waiting for someone to eat them. When anyone verbalized how hard and crusty they had become, Enid's replied, "I love them."

There was constant reminder that Enid's family survived the hardships of prairie pioneer life because of their strong Scottish spirit and thrift. Her insistence suited Walter. His Teutonic German blood reveled in the strength of both hard work and thrift. Marriage between German and British nationalities brought together two cultures with the same values; however, sometimes the values were reversed in priority. The Scottish heritage's first priority was education. In the German way of thinking, education was last in priority when it came to use of money due to doubt that the investment would return very much money. When there was disagreement Walter reminded, "Don't make a mountain out of a molehill."

CHAPTER 8
Iowa the Tall Corn State

When autumn began wagons came back from the cornfield full of corn. When the corn was put into cribs, German Grandpa Henry Krug watched for large full ears which were tossed into bushel baskets and carried to the second floor of the farmhouse to sort and carefully lay them out to dry. Several kernels from each ear were taken and moistened and laid in a tray to incubate and germinate. When kernels did not sprout, the ears from which they were taken were fed to the hogs and chickens. The ears from kernels that germinated were shelled and used for seed to plant the next year's crop.

In the mid-20th century new hybrid patented seed corn was purchased in sacks each year by Iowa farmers to increase the yields beyond anything Grandpa Henry Krug thought possible at the turn of the 20th century. The need to increase corn production during the years of World War II was a boom to the acceptance and use of patented hybrid seed corn and its development.

It was very important to rotate crops. Corn was raised two years in the same field, next the field was sown to oats and seeded down for alfalfa hay for several years using a five year plan. Sometimes a field was left in grain longer than two years to increase feed for the cattle and hogs. When the government acreage program came in, fields were left in alfalfa for three years even though some farmers put in government acres for only one year. It cost so much to seed alfalfa that often a field in hay was left for three years.

Soybeans were not raised at that time on Krug farms and there was none of the watershed erosion that results when soybeans loosened the soil resulting in grass roots that never established in the soil again. In later years it was corn and soybeans—alternate years, and alfalfa seed only two years in a row. Soybeans had to be bone dry to store them.

The goal of the corn crop in hand picking days of the first forty years of the 20th century was to complete the harvest by Thanksgiving Day. When my sister and I were home from school, and on weekends, it was our chore to ride in the horse drawn wagon box and level the corn when it bounced off the bangboard from toss of the hand pickers. The horses, trained to follow our father's voice command while he continued picking corn by hand, moved ahead in the corn rows until they were hollered at. The horses' sudden movement made the wagon lurch forward in the rough furrows of soil between the corn rows. Children's arms and legs soon filled with bruises either from falling into the mounting corn when the wagon jolted, or from being hit by ears of corn thrown by the pickers as corn bounced off the bangboard. The hard ear corn kernels pierced skin drawing blood when corn ears hit the body.

When picking corn by hand, Walter and Enid would take three rows between them. At an Uncle's farm, there was no elevator so all corn had to be scooped off the wagon again into the crib. It was much easier to pick the corn than to scoop it off because of the weight. It usually took five to six weeks, as a rule, to pick the corn crop.

Corn-picking started early in the morning, 5 a.m. – 5:30 a.m. Schedule: go to the barn, feed the horses, get the cows in, feed and milk them, separate the milk, feed the calves skim milk, slop the hogs, harness the horses, go to the house and eat breakfast, hitch up the horses, go out to the field and pick a load of corn by noon. The plan was to get a load of corn out of the field by 11:30 a.m. so it could be unloaded during the lunch hour. In the afternoon, the schedule was to pick one load of corn, unload, do the chores of milking, and other work. A corn "mishill" brought happiness because that meant it was faster to go through the field.

A former Kansas farmer living in rural Atkins, who lost everything in the "Great Depression," was hired for corn picking. His work was liked because he was fast and a good 'corn picker' and was also hired whenever the family went on vacation to do all the farm chores. In the 1940's the farm had to be tended up to three weeks at a time when the family traveled to Salt Lake City to visit Grandpa Bryner.

Walter did not often hire help for corn picking because the corn did not spoil. He always hoped to have the corn out of the field before the first snowfall of the season. The last ear of corn was always tossed twenty-five to thirty feet in the air with the exclamation, "Here's the one I've been looking for all year!"

One year, both Walter and Enid picked corn on Thanksgiving Day instead of going to church. The next day there was more than two and a half feet of snow on the ground from a blizzard that raged during the night. They were very thankful that year they had finished picking the corn crop on Thanksgiving Day instead of going to church.

The market price for corn was raised from fifteen cents a bushel in 1931 to $2.65 a bushel in the 1960's. In 1971, corn production tripled due to hybrid seed corn, better weed control, and better fertilizer. In some cases, production quadrupled. The alfalfa crop became ten times as large as it was in the early years of the century. The practice of spreading lime on the farm was followed every seven years for more than thirty years. The first year lime was spread on only four acres, and the acres were sowed to alfalfa the next year.

Every November Grandpa Henry Krug held a "settling up" night after the corn harvest was complete. The farming business that night was conducted in the German language only and Walter did not tell Enid what was said. An agreement was reached with each son about the rent owed and was adjusted according to the crops produced on the land during the year. In 1931 and 1932, Walter did not pay rent because he did not have an income. The extended family farming business was conducted behind closed doors by only the immediate men of the family, Grandpa Henry Krug and his four sons. In-laws did not know anything about it or have a word to say about any of it.

When the meeting was over, Enid always inquired of Walter if he was satisfied, and his answer was unhesitatingly and emphatically, "Yes!" Nothing more was ever said about that important annual night of farming business. The women in-laws laid plans for a late night supper that was held after the meeting. While the meeting was going on the women gathered in another room and caught up on gossip. The children played in an upstairs room and "ran wild" as it was later described.

The red barn on the farm had *W. W. Krug* painted in white and a line beneath it with the 1910 date it was built. The old red corncrib had the year 1912 painted in white on the end facing the road. A new corncrib was built in 1941 at a cost of $300 and completed in time for the corn harvest that season. Grandpa Henry Krug lived with Walter's family all during the building process. He smoked cigarettes and one day when he was lighting his cigarette in the dining room, a cool breeze blew through the windows and started his mustache on fire. He then shaved it off. The family always remembered this "trimming" of Grandpa's mustache!

Walter and an older brother went together to purchase their first mechanical cornpicker the winter of 1940. They bought it from their Uncle August Happel, Happel & Sons Implement Company, Cedar Rapids, at a cost of $750.00 for taking it out to our farm and storing it until the fall harvest season. New corn pickers ordinarily cost $1,100.00-$1,200.00 in season. Walter's youngest brother bought into the partnership in time for the autumn cornpicking season.

Walter purchased a mounted cornpicker in 1951 and traded in the old one. He was the sole owner of the new mounted machine. He also traded in his fifteen year old Oliver 70 tractor for an Oliver 77 with starter, rubber tires, lights, and power lift at a cost of $2,195.00. It was sold on his 1966 farm retirement auction for $780.00.

In 1952 Walter bought a tractor-corn planter, tractor manure spreader, and tractor mower. A cultipacker and mulcher was used in the 1950's and 1960's to bust clods of dirt after plowing or before planting corn. This machinery would bust clods of soil a disk had never been able to break. (Corn combines came in after Walter quit farming.)

The tractor manure spreader was again traded in on a power-take-off spreader, $800.00 with trade-in, and sold at his 1966 farm retirement auction for $375.00. All farm machinery was switched completely from horse to tractor from 1950-52.

Horses were used until 1952 to plant corn, mow hay, rake hay and haul manure after tractors were owned. A team of horses named "King" and "Queen" were the last team Walter owned. They were a large pair of sorrels and he paid $275.00 for them. They proved to be run-away horses several times and he sold them for $190.00 to a buyer from Boston, Massachusetts.

"Go to the house!" Walter scolded. He preferred not having children around when he was working. Children liked to run up to him when he was watering the horses at the tank in the farm yard, whereupon he promptly taught rules of safety which he enforced. Children never dared walk or stand behind the horses or they could be kicked. Children could not stand in front of the horses or they might scare them with their quick movements. Horses were very sensitive to talk and any movements necessary in their farm work.

It became important to gradually increase the Holstein herd of milking cows to get a larger weekly cream check to buy more groceries and pay out of the pocket expenses. Grade A butterfat was marketed at the Wapsie Valley Creamery. It was important to get the highest possible prices for milk, and Walter was very fussy about how the cows were milked and how the milk was run through the separator. He poured the pails of warm milk into the large separator bowl that had two spouts. He turned a handle until one spout had cream coming out of it and skim milk came out of the other spout. He fed the skimmed milk to the hogs.

It was Enid's job to daily wash the forty-five parts of the cream separator with boiling hot water and rinse it with more boiling water. The skimmed separated milk, the by-product of the dairy herd, was a main part of the hog's diet along with corn to fatten them, producing a second source of income from the livestock. When hogs reached prime weight, they were sent to market.

Walter's farming business increased by feeding corn to feeder cattle that were bought instead of increasing the milking herd. The first Herford cattle he bought from western range land were purchased in the Kansas City Stockyards from a man working for a commission in Kansas City. Walter drove to Kansas City where he bought forty-five head of Hereford cattle and shipped them by train to Atkins. It was possible to ship a carload of cattle and sidetrack it on one of the ten tracks across from his farm. He then drove the cattle from the railroad car across to his farm. He had permission from the neighbor, his German Happel cousin, to open their barbed wire fence so he could drive the cattle from the railroad across their field. He continued to buy feeder cattle in Kansas City for four years and while there stayed in a hotel on Stockman's rates.

The cattle were fed for nine months on ground corn. The first years the cattle were sold to a Waterloo, Iowa, packing house. The best year was 1952-53 when the cattle were purchased at a little over 300 pounds each. When sold in Waterloo they weighed almost 1,100 pounds each. For fifty Herefords $10,000-$11,000 was made on them.

In later years, the corn crop was fed to the cattle and they were shipped to the Chicago Stockyards that proved to be more profitable than cribbing the corn and waiting for a price to shell the corn and sell it to the local grain elevator. Walter's cattle graded prime beef on the Chicago market and brought him much satisfaction for his labor and investment.

He trucked the cattle to the Chicago Stockyards and accompanied them until they were sold. He had to pay for feeding the cattle in Chicago until the sale was complete.

The commission men got the bids on the cattle. Walter stayed at the Stockyards Inn and ate meals in the Chicago Livestock Exchange building. When he received his check for the cattle from the commission men, they sent him back to his Iowa farm by private limousine.

There were times on the farm whenWalter showed his family his cattle. They walked across the pasture to look at them and then helped him drive them home to the watering tank. He was proud of the cattle. When he stopped walking, he pointed out those that he especially thought were outstanding. Walking down the lane that ran from the barnyard to the back forty acres he paused to show off his corn crop. He was very proud of the tall stalks of corn.

"That's green gold you're looking at. Green gold!" was Walter's description of acres and acres of dark green corn fields. The wealth of the crop could not be accurately determined until fall harvest, but the bounty of beauty of the growing corn was a wealth in itself. The shaping of land as rich as Iowa, where more than one crop comes out of the soil, produced men and women of sterling character and inflexible resolution. Life in the tall corn state, on the great plains of Iowa, was not only one of toil, it was achievement.

Walter never talked about what the corn crop produced in terms of dollars because corn was fed into the beef cattle to produce prime beef prices, and corn was fed into hogs to produce several truck loads to go to the market each year, and corn was ground to make feed for the horses, cows, and chickens. The remainder of the corn crop was shelled and sold before the next crop was harvested to make space in the corncrib. Some years the cribbed corn was sealed on a U.S. government program and that increased the dollars received for that crop.

PART III

*My heart will keep and ponder the things
in this hour of grace.*

PART II.

*heat, light, and gender-bending
... the last of energy*

CHAPTER 9
Extended Family Years

Every Iowa summer the large extended Krug, Happel, Werning, Moeller German families held a reunion in a Cedar Rapids park where there was a pavilion that held large picnic groups. World War II gas rationing prevented the large annual extended family picnic from taking place. It was long enough before the war years ceased that the very large extended family reunion was never restarted again.

First Christmas Day, December 25, was for the individual family celebration; second Christmas Day, December 26, was family reunion day with grandparents and first cousins; third Christmas Day was for friends and other related family reunions.

The holidays were a busy time for extended family life. Children were kept busy cleaning the house to be ready for company. There were gifts to wrap that included ironing the gift wrapping paper that had been carefully saved from the opening of gifts from the previous year. Gift wrapping paper in the 1930's and 1940's was made with a rag content and wrinkles and bends in it could be ironed out carefully with an iron that was not too hot. Scissors were used to straighten the torn edges, but most family members were careful in opening gifts so as not to tear the paper too much. Some pieces were used year after year and they became smaller each time with more straightening of the used edges. With the careful saving of wrapping paper it was possible to have favorite wrapping papers on gifts.

Walter and Enid gave stockings, a handkerchief and a picture to longtime neighbor friends. Those friends sent Walter and Enid a gift subscription to the *Christian Herald* each year with the inscription: "To add to your inspiration throughout the coming year, *Christian Herald* is to be sent to you as a gift—for we have seen his star in the East, and have come to worship him." Matthew 2:2.

Scottish Great-Grandma Groff and Grandma Bryner were Christmas Day dinner guests at Enid and Walter's farm. Walter constructed a doll house before Christmas and under the Christmas tree on Christmas morning were five sets of doll furniture to furnish the doll house. Every second Christmas Day, December 26, a reunion was held of Grandpa Henry Krug's extended family with everyone in attendance. Grandpa Henry Krug furnished the meat and his five children's families furnished the remainder of the meal. New Year's Day dinner Walter and Enid's family spent with Great-Grandma Groff and Grandma Bryner at their home in Cedar Rapids, Iowa.

President FDR Roosevelt's Thanksgiving Day was observed in 1939 on November 23. Children were in school all that day. A roasted dressing stuffed chicken was dinner that evening. November 30, the National Thanksgiving Day, the menu was again roasted chicken and dressing with gravy and going to church in the evening. An aunt brought Grandma Bryner to the farm on December 24th to go to Christmas Eve services and to stay overnight for Christmas Day.

Card playing was the common activity in the German extended families during holidays and winter months when there was not as much daytime work on the farm. Chores could be finished earlier in the afternoon and adults were willing to stay up later in the evening for social gatherings. Both men and women played and the winning individuals rotated to the next table with scores computed during the evening. Prizes were given for the highest individual score and also for the lowest score, called "the booby prize." The frequent card players of the extended family took their games seriously and played to win. Grandpa Henry Krug never learned to play cards during his lifetime. He watched the game, but was not a player. His generation's social life evolved around relative home dinner visitation.

President Roosevelt's Thanksgiving Day was November 21 in 1940. Schools were in session all day. The National Thanksgiving in America was November 28. Grandpa Henry Krug came to Walter and Enid's home to eat dinner and went to church with them in the evening.

World War II 1942 Thanksgiving-- Grandma Bryner came on the bus on US Hwy 30 to the Atkins highway corner where Walter met her and also drove her home the day after the holiday. Grandma Bryner came home with the family from a shopping and marketing trip on December 24th and enjoyed going to the Christmas Eve program at the church. New Year's Day was spent at Grandma Bryner's home for dinner and then a drive home in a blizzard that afternoon.

World War II 1943, Thanksgiving, November 25, Grandma Bryner came on the bus to US Hwy 30 Atkins corner. Enid had three stuffed Guinea hens and dressing on the menu. New Year's Eve was spent at Krug cousins after going to evening church service followed by card playing and eating of lots of popcorn, candy, sandwiches, cake, cookies and homemade ice-cream until 4:00 a.m. New Year's Day we went to Grandma Bryners for dinner.

World War II 1944 was a snowy white Christmas Eve and Day. Enid took roast duck stuffed with dressing to Grandma Bryner's home for evening supper and the family stayed until after midnight. New Year's Eve was again church service followed by going again to a Krug cousin's home to eat and play cards, eat a freezer of homemade ice-cream, pumpkin and chocolate pies. Playing cards occupied time while watching the New Year come in.

In the 20th century, Iowa German extended families were engaged in diversified farming on an increasingly mechanized basis. Children were expected to share farm responsibilities to further the goals of farming the land. Young children could help every day by carrying wood for the cook stove or furnace; pumping soft water from the rain water cistern to fill the reservoir on the back of the cook stove; pumping hard water from the deep well to fill a drinking pail for household use; carrying corn cobs to keep the kindling basket full; rounding up the cattle for watering and stantioning in the barn; feeding and watering the chickens and ducks, and gathering eggs; throwing corn to the hogs in the pigyard; and carrying the empty milk pails to the barn to be ready for milking time.

As soon as children survived all the highly contagious diseases siblings brought home from school, that often began with a severe case of whooping cough that required the calling of a doctor to the farm home and was followed by mumps and "pink eye," and a severe case of red measles, there were farm chores to be done at a young age when it was difficult to climb over the fences to gather eggs in the cattle shed where nests were built for hens to lay their eggs when they were foraging on grain dropped by the cattle.

Instructions were given about always gathering eggs before dusk and before the chickens went to roost. It was important to climb into the barn haymow before dark to be better able to see where the nests of eggs were hidden. That made it necessary to climb the hand-over-hand ladder to the haymow and figure out a way to manage both the ladder and an egg pail filled with eggs at the same time on the descent. It resulted in cracked or broken eggs at times. Lowering down the steep ladder, hand over hand with a full pail of eggs was difficult, especially when the haymow was so full with hay sticking through the chute that there was little crawling space. That is just where the hens got into the haymow and hid their nests.

In desperation, when the haymow was jammed full of hay and the chute narrow, it was important to make sure there was a huge pile of hay at the bottom of the ladder before beginning the climb to get the eggs. After the pail was carefully filled with eggs that were stacked evenly together so they would not jiggle, the pail was dropped from the top of the haymow to fall into the big pile of soft hay. It worked. Fewer eggs were cracked or broken by this method than when an attempt was made to lower oneself, requiring the use of both hands, while trying to balance the egg pail on an arm at the same time. It was the only way to also prevent falling down the chute when trying to save the eggs in the bucket.

Sometimes there was a warning ahead of time that at least two or more buckets were needed to gather all the eggs in the haymow. Beside the haymow, it was necessary to look for eggs in the horses feed boxes, the cow feeding stantions, and the boxes nailed by the calf feeding pens.

"What happened, so many broken eggs?" Walter sometimes noticed the buckets of yolk spattered eggs in the house basement before Enid had time to clean and grade them.

"Let me answer. Don't talk about what happened to the eggs," Enid warned. She took full responsibility for the number of eggs that went to market, and when she finished talking with Walter nothing more was ever said about broken eggs. More than once she said, "The hens are breaking eggs again." That seemed to stop all the questions. The chicken house usually needed cleaning, delousing, and the roosts sprayed and Walter's inquiries became a prediction of a cleaner chicken house within a short time.

A good laying hen of 60-70% production would lay eggs a little over 200 days a year. Double yolk eggs caused ruptures in the laying hen. When hens started to complete their yearly cycle, they started laying medium and small size eggs and they started to go into a moult. They moulted for sixty days, lost feathers, gained weight, and grew new feathers. The chickens did not all moult at the same time. Extremely hot and extremely cold weather slowed down the moulting process. In cold weather chickens utilized most of the feed for warmth and there were few eggs. Warm water helped them lay more eggs in cold weather. The real hot weather of summer months put the chickens into a moult. The two year old hens quit laying in the summer months when the weather was hot and did not lay again until the following spring, about February. A year old hen would lay eggs if it was well taken care of in the summer months.

It was necessary to crawl over fences to reach some nests, sometimes with two buckets, that were partially filled with eggs. Many times cracked or broken eggs happened in the process of negotiating a fence, especially in icy and snowy weather.

The cattle shed required climbing over two fences and crossing a deep manure area of the cattle yard to reach the loafing shed. Sometimes there were slippery icy patches in the sloping barnyard when crossed from one building to another. There was a time when both feet slipped all at once, when there was a nearly full pail of eggs in each hand. Fortunately it was possible to land in a snow bank and so did all the eggs. They flew out of the dropping pail. Sometimes the messy pails and what was left of the eggs that could be salvaged could be taken to the house, and sometimes when all was lost it was just necessary to continue on the egg gathering rounds and wait to tell Enid what had happened when all finished gathering for the day. She could easily see from the yolk spattered remains that there had been an accident.

Enid never scolded me even though eggs were her source of spending money. She simply always inquired about any injuries that may have happened in the processt. The refrigerator was always full of cracked eggs that were used in cooking meals and baking. They were also fried and made into sandwiches for lunch.

When the egg check increased, Walter gave Enid only part of it. He used the rest of it for weekly groceries or out-of-the-pocket expenses. He did not part with money once he got his hands on it. It was an obsession to conserve every penny for the farm business. Saving money was more important than family pleasure, or anything else.

"You need someone on your side," Grandma Bryner said many times when she spent time on the farm. "When can we gather eggs? Grandma asked anxiously looking forward to that farm chore. She recalled happy memories of days when she and Grandpa Bryner owned and farmed different farms, three in Iowa and one in Wisconsin.

"Do you mind if I gather some of the eggs?" Grandma asked. She took the pail and reached under the hens in the nests. She paused in the cow barn to talk with Walter and tell him how much she liked to drink warm milk. He obliged her and made sure there was a pitcher of fresh warm milk taken to the house for Grandma to drink that evening. When the supply of milk ran low for Enid's cooking, Walter brought in fresh milk before it had cooled in the morning for breakfast or in the evening for supper. The fresh warm milk tasted just like the smell of cow urine. Milk products actually are smelled and not tasted according to dairy judging teams who were being trained so the judgement about tasting like cow urine was accurate. Fresh warm milk was one of the things Grandma Bryner really liked. There was plenty of time to smell cow urine doing chores, or when bringing up the cattle from the pasture, herding cows and locking them in the cow yards.

"A penny for your thoughts," Grandma Bryner broke the silence. When nothing was said, she repeatedly wanted to know what her grandchild was thinking.

"Nothing," was the reply.

Grandma refused to give up trying to start talking with grandchildren. "Your father's a good man." Grandma Bryner said it many times though she understood that father had his own way of doing things. She knew he was exacting and demanding about farm work.

"Your mother works too hard," Grandma Bryner said on every farm visit. "She has your father's German relatives standing on the back porch much of the time." It was true. One of his brother's often came during mealtime to call father to the closed-in porch to discuss a work issue on one of the family farms. That was the time of day they knew they could find him and he would take time to talk. Always, it seemed, one of them came when Grandma Bryner was visiting the farm. The back door of the kitchen to the porch was always closed to those porch conversations regardless of the weather. Nothing stopped those often times lengthy conversations. It was was the life of an extended farming family.

"I never had to work as hard as your mother when I lived on a farm" Grandma Bryner reminisced about her farming life. She never talked about that in front of her daughter Enid. She tried to help her understand in the process of her explanation. "We had new homes and all new furniture everywhere we lived," Grandma Bryner continued, however, she usually mentioned how much she regretted filing for divorce from Grandpa Bryner when she was fifty years old.

Walter remembered that when he started farming in the "Great Depression" years he did not have an income from the farm for two years. He never got over that fact. It was in the worst of the "Great Depression" years and he could not even send his hogs to the slaughter house. They were not buying them. Instead of destroying the hogs, as the government advocated, those on Grandpa Krug's extended family farms were butchered and the meat canned for future consumption. Drought hit the potato crop and potatoes had to be purchased for two years.

"We'll buy you what you need, when you need it," Walter insisted instead of giving children a spending allowance. He sometimes did things that indulged in his own interest and pleasure. The day he came home from a farm auction with an old bobsled with runners on it for use in snow Enid asked, "What are you going to do with that?" Silence followed. Later, in listening through the floor register in one of the upstairs bedrooms above the breakfast table, the conversation between parents, the only time each day the two of them spent time together by themselves without any children around, he could be heard saying he just wanted the bobsled because he would like to have it for nostalgia reasons. He parked it on the dirt floor of the machine shed and there it remained all his years on the farm. He never took it out and used it, not even in winter.

Many Saturday evenings, Walter changed clothing, after eating supper, and went to rural Atkins to the one block long main street of stores. He went to the local barbershop and had his hair cut. When overheard talking early Sunday morning, over breakfast, the two of them were discussing the latest news of the community. The local barbershop was the social center for the men of the community. Any needed groceries were bought on those Saturday night jaunts while waiting for a turn in the barber chair.

The social life of a German family centered on visits to and from our extended German family and birthday parties. We celebrated Great-Grandma "Nettie"Groff's birthday every year with a dinner at her lovely Cedar Rapids home high on a bluff of the Cedar River. A story and photo about her age appeared each year in the *Cedar Rapids Gazette* newspaper. Those visits frequently extended into chore time on the farm and there was impatience to leave the city and "start for home."

"Come now, let's go!" Walter urged, irritation showing in his voice when it was not the first time he had made that suggestion. He waited for the children to start toward the front door.

"We're not through yet," Enid pleaded having learned she could extend time a little; extra minutes that she enjoyed so much with her family.

The German language was used by the men of the Krug family when they gathered together as long as Walter's brothers were alive. Walter outlived all of them. His sister's husband descended from one of the earliest German families to migrate to the Benton County area, and had acculturated by his generation in that he spoke only English during his lifetime. Grandpa Krug's grandchildren always worried about that Uncle during family reunions because he always stood with his hands behind his back, with a grin on his face, and listened in on the children's conversations. Was that Uncle listening for bits of news about the individual families from hearing the children's talking, or was he probably just interested in what he was hearing. The children always wished he would stay with the men in their gathering though it was quite impossible, since he was no longer bilingual.

Enid lived all her life in a seventeen mile area of Benton and Linn County, Iowa. The wives of Walter's many cousins were involved in driving to the same meetings she attended, therefore, she found plenty of opportunities for transportation to everything she wanted to go to even though she never learned to drive a car. She was a leader in organizing women's meetings of the local farm organization that sponsored educational activities for the ladies of the township. Enid had more education than the women of Walter's extended family and they could all benefit from the educational opportunities she helped organize.

The neighbors of Grandpa and Grandma Henry Krug were the parents of Enid's "best chum" from her Washington High School days in Cedar Rapids. "That's how I met your father," mother reminded. An invitation to Enid from that neighbor's eldest daughter to go on a summer picnic with two of the next farm neighbor Krug brothers blossomed into a two year acquaintance and romance culminating in the marriage of Walter and Enid.

"Hurry! Grab your food basket. Your ride is here!" it was necessary to call upstairs to where Enid was dressing in the master bedroom, changing from the work clothing she styled and sewed in her favorite patchwork design. The master bedroom closet was the only clothing storage in our farmhouse, a walk-in closet where Walter's wardrobe of winter and summer business suits, and Enid's wedding dress of silk hung along with the best dresses she wore when leaving the farm.

"Tell Arlene I'll be right there!"Enid yelled. She relied on Walter's cousins to take her to meetings. Enid's lack of driving, therefore, lack of transportation never slowed her social life. She liked to get away from the work of the farm and was not shy about taking action by phoning one of Walter's relatives. She frequently rode with the wife of one of Walter's cousins who she had known since going to high school in Cedar Rapids.

"Hurry! If you talk when you pick up Daisy, you'll be late," was yelled up the staircase again as the time passed.

Enid descended the stairs, grabbed the potluck basket, placed it over her right arm and picked up her purse in the other hand. Social time with food was a regular part of the women's meetings. Enid baked two, three, four or more pies each time she made pastry depending upon how many functions she had on the schedule requiring her to take food. She found a pie was easy to carry away from home and women liked pie. In summer months the women met in the afternoon. In winter, the women met at twelve o'clock starting with dinner and several men who helped with transportation also stayed for the noon meal.

All her life Enid attended what was originally organized as the Women's Foreign Missionary Society in 1874. Several of Enid's Cedar Rapids high school friends who married German relatives attended the afternoon once-a-month meetings. Scripture reading, singing and prayer were the purpose of the women to meet over all the years. Each meeting ended with refreshments, tea and coffee, cake, pie or fruit sauce, pickles and cheese, and cold sliced meat. None were considered obligatory, but tea or coffee and biscuits and butter. The Fairview little, white, rural church, where the women first met, closed in late 1923.

Meetings continued in homes of the members the second Tuesday of each month. The women took turns conducting the devotional service. Each member paid one dollar annual dues and dropped a free will offering in the Mite Box and side dish for penny collection at each meeting. Membership averaged twenty-five to thirty women of different faiths. The group could well have been called the Fairview Society of Sisterly Love. Cards and flowers were sent to the sick and bereaved. Contributions were made to the Home for the Aged, Linn and Benton County Retarded Children's Homes, The Board of World Relief, American Bible Society, The Red Cross, and to Camp Good Health. Each meeting closed with singing, "When the roll is called up yonder I'll be there," and, "Blest be the tie that binds our hearts in Christian love; the fellowship of kindred minds is like to that above."

We were always in close contact with the neighbors of the Henry Krug grandparents during harvesting and we made winter social visits to their home. Another of the neighbor's sayings always remembered, "A good neighbor is the same as a relative." That was always followed by laughter in the most contented way.

Walter's extended German family gathered together and pooled labor for some tasks such as the making of sorgum. A Krug great-uncle had the Krug family cooking vat and press on his farm. This is how they made molasses:

"The cane sorgum was stripped (leaves taken off), tops cut off, and loaded into wagons to transport it to Uncle's farm. The cane was unloaded one day, the next day we ground juice out of it. A horse on a power wheel turned the roller or cane press that squeezed the juices out. We cleaned out the pressed up stocks and cooked the molasses. We burnt a lot of wood under the vat, pretty good sized chunks of wood. It took 5-6-7 hours of cooking. We evaporated the water out of it by stirring, skimmed the top off to remove the scum, ending up with less than twenty gallons of molasses from one vat full of juice. We took cream cans to put the cooked molasses in to transport it home. Then we filled stone crocks and stored the molasses in the upstairs unused, unheated in winter, bedroom of our farm house."

Children liked eating molasses candy made in fresh fallen snow. Following a snow storm molasses was taken from the large crocks in the upstairs storeroom and dropped by tablespoons full into fresh clean fallen snow. It would stiffen rapidly and could be picked up in the hand and chewed like candy drops. This was a special treat for children to eat from the freshly made molasses. Cane sorgum is a field crop that grows in the same soil as the field corn in Iowa.

The younger generation in the extended German families learned at a young age what was wise to do and what was foolish when Enid read to them the Aesop-like fables that she used in teaching. Work ethic and agrarian values were taught through stories about an ant and a grasshopper:

> "In a field one day a grasshopper was hopping about chirping and singing. An ant passed by, pulling a grain of corn. 'Why not come and skip with me,' said the grasshopper, 'instead of toiling all day long?' 'I am helping to lay up food for winter,' said the ant, 'and you should do the same.'" The ant went on toiling, and pulled grain after grain of corn to the nest. The grasshopper skipped about and chirped. When winter came, the grasshopper had no food. Hungry and cold, he came to the ant to ask for something to eat. Then the ant said to him, 'If you had worked when I did, instead of skipping about, you would not be hungry."

"Which proverb to you think fits the story?" Enid asked, "A penny saved is a penny earned. A rolling stone gathers no moss. Make hay while the sun shines."

"That's easy," my sister answered. "Make hay while the sun shines."

Mother also told the fable about a country girl:

> A country girl was walking along the road with a pail of milk on her head. She was saying to herself, 'The money I shall get for this milk will buy me three hundred eggs. These eggs will

hatch as many chickens. The chickens will be fit to carry to market about Christmas, and they will bring a good sum. I shall have money enough to buy a new dress. In this dress I shall go to the fair, where all the boys will think me a pretty maid, but I shall pass them proudly by! With this she tossed her head. Over went the pail, and all the milk was spilled on the ground!"

Enid asked children to guess which proverb fit the story: "Don't cry over spilt milk or Don't count your chickens before they hatch?"

My sister answered right away, "Don't cry over spilt milk."

One of the earliest memories of Walter's older brother was his talking in a funny sound, his German brogue preceding every syllable. This delighted children and it was amusing that he could not pronounce the letter "y." He always spoke about the lard light instead of yard light. He was married to a rather forbidding woman whose bosom always preceded her into a room. This uncle was not an intimidating person. He knew nothing but hard work, and he did more work all his life than any other member of our Krug extended family. He never walked. He had a running gait at all times. He was not happy unless he was working. His happiest times were when he was working with a brother on either his or one of the Krug farms.

This was my German uncle who could, like Grandpa Henry Krug, tell family history and had a perfect memory of family dates. He was the first of the Krug brothers to die. His death came at haymaking time, the result of an accidental fall from the top of a very high load of hay he stacked too high and was hauling to the barn on his farm. He, like his brothers, fought the hard battle of the "Great Depression" of the twentieth century and won. They never gave up the hope they had in their heart that everything would get better. They believed all things are possible for corn farmers who work hard. Believers are winners. The German Krug brother's green corn fields turned into real gold. They believed in the God who made them, the Savior who saved them, and the immorality of the soul.

Enid's expertise in handling children, a result of her professional training and experience as an elementary teacher in Iowa public schools before her marriage, had a kindly manner that showed through in her love and appreciation of her own children. Like all American parents, she had a dream for her children. Not all parents want a future president of the nation in the family, but they dream that their children will have good friends, a pleasant home, and a successful way to make a living.

PART IV

One who does not toil for his country will give up oneself.

CHAPTER 10
Years of Change

The changing cycle of the seasons: spring plowing, sowing, planting, cultivating, haymaking, threshing, harvesting; fall plowing—a continuous farm cycle year after year for Iowa German-Scottish American families. Aging farm buildings and farm machinery changed with the advancement of technology. The horse-age gave way to the machine age. The ousting of the horse by the tractor and self-propelled machinery transformed Iowa summer farming and rural life. Change was everywhere as rising industrialization began converting the nation's agrarian economy into an industrial society.

By the end of World War II the measure of a progressive farmer was the amount of production he accomplished each year. The use of lime to prevent depletion of the soil from heavy cropping and growth of alfalfa and clover cover crops were common to add nitrogen to the soil and reduce erosion and weeds. Corn crops were rotated with oats and alfalfa on a three year cycle to increase the corn yield and replenish the soil after the corn harvest.

Fields were fenced so cattle could graze in the fields after haymaking in years when fields were rotated to alfafa and clover crops. Milkweed and wild roses sometimes grew in the fence lines. Canadian thistles were a constant menance in every field every year. The greatest change in farming came with the use of commercial fertilizers, insecticides and herbicides that fouled streams and polluted groundwater while increasing the grain yield to record highs.

Life for German-Scottish families in USA originally centered on family dinner exchanges, summer reunion picnics, harvest-help exchanges, winter time card party socials, church gatherings for weddings, baptisms, confirmations, anniversaries, and funeral wakes. The families valued the observance of these traditional gatherings for generations until Americanization, and the end of their spoken native German language, permeated the depths of "Old World" roots to the extent that the younger generations forgot their German and Scottish heritage for these activities.

After Christina Krug's death, Henry Krug held a farm sale to dispose of all of her household possessions and of his farm machinery. He turned his farm over to his youngest son and invested the money received from the sale. The Krug family had the faith to struggle, the belief to survive and triumph, with hope and trust in the reliability of God in a world of change. Even though people changed and farming changed, the Krug family found that the soil remained the same.

Enid bought one of German Christina Krug's high board, hand-carved beds for the spare room in the five bedroom farmhouse. Grandpa Henry Krug slept in it when he stayed on the farm to help with the work, or did carpentry work on buildings. Enid also purchased the tall glass-door china closet and six caned seat, carved wheat design, dining room chairs that were part of Christina's dowry when she married Henry Krug before the turn of the century. Nobody bid on Christina's dishes or silver coffee service, both wedding presents in 1898, so Enid bid on them and got them for "little or nothing." In later years, Enid explained that many relatives attended the auction, and when they saw the immediate family biding on an item the others did not put in a bid. That was the only way it was possible to determine placement of items of family sentimental value when everything was sold at public auction.

Enid also bought the pressed glass dishes and silver gravy ladle that were the Henry Krug grandparent's 25th wedding anniversary presents. When Enid told who they once belonged to, it was always enjoyable getting them out of the china cupboard, polishing them and helping set the table for company dinners or harvester meals. They were the only association that remained with Grandma Christina Krug who died in 1934 before the younger generation could remember her.

Grandpa and Grandma Henry Krug, like their immigrant parents before them, prospered in Iowa farming. Great-Great Grandfather Johann Justus Krug III brought the original family from Löhlbach, Germany to Iowa and only lived fourteen years in America. He died on the Krug homestead he purchased six months after arriving in Iowa. Eldest son John Krug lived all his life and died on that Krug homestead. In his lifetime he added acreage to increase the size of the farm. He also went into banking with other German immigrants and prospered enabling him to place each of his six sons on a farm that became their life work. His youngest son then farmed the Krug homestead. Years later, his grandson continued to farm it.

Both Christina and Henry Krug were the oldest of ten children in their family. There were one-hundred first cousins even though there was a batchelor uncle in each of the Krug and Happel families. As changes in farming occurred, Krug men had less time away from the demands of their farm operation. Family life changed as Henry Krug's extended family farming changed, but the values of courage, compassion and faith prevailed. Individual families of the extended unit sought change, and a different life style. There was less and less social interaction among the German families as changes occurred.

In rainy or inclement summer weather Grandpa Henry Krug spent the days straightening and sorting nails. His constant pounding on a piece of flat iron could be heard all around the farmyard. When he was not sorting nails he was sorting used lumber. Every one of his farms had piles of lumber he had carefully sorted and saved for future building projects. Nothing was ever thrown away or discarded lest it be needed at a future time in his carpentry work.

Everyone in the family looked forward to summer weekends when Enid always had a travel idea for something that would be away from the farm in good weather. Her favorite of Walter's relatives was a cousin's wife of Swedish nationality with whom a social exchange was developed, and they shared common frugal management when it came to food and spending money.

The two women planned family outings on the spur of the moment when the cousin's wife, older and well organized would say, "You make a dish of salad and I'll make one. You pack some sandwiches for your family and I'll do the same for my family. If you bake a pie, I'll bake a cake and we can go for a Sunday drive together." The menu was often similar and the two families enjoyed each other's company and a day of travel to a state park or place of common interest. It was the simple and frugal kind of planning that mother liked best. A favorite 4th of July holiday outing was a drive to northern Iowa to Clear Lake for the holiday time where the children could swim while the adults fished much of the time.

Clear Lake Iowa: (left to right)
Albert Krug, Margaret Krug, Elaine Krug

Clear Lake Iowa: (left to right)
Elaine Krug, Margaret Krug, Albert Krug

Walter fed cattle until an accident happened when bales of hay fell on him in the hay mow on a cold winter night as he was feeding the cattle. The vertebras in his neck were damaged by the weight of the bales of hay. He entered the hospital and the doctor advised him to retire from farming. Thereafter, he built a retirement home in Atkins on A Avenue and moved into it in 1966; it was located one mile from his farm. It was a change for Walter for which farming was life itself; the soil, the feel of the earth and the great respect he had for it. He often picked up a handful of soil after he had worked up a field and felt how loose it was and free from clods, ready for another crop. He liked the feel of the soil and he liked to walk on it. He liked the good clean earth.

Enid, having been raised in the city, became a farmer's wife who could think out and do the economical thing. She liked and preferred the privacy of living on a farm compared to having her neighbors always know what she was always doing when she retired and moved into a rural town. There was security on the land when living on a farm.

The memory of European life faded rapidly with the dying of immigrant generations and the pursuit of "the American Dream" became the reality of life for the younger generations of families in the developing nation.

CHAPTER 11
Connecting With The Past

Grandpa Henry Krug's talk about "our home" in Germany was constant and never forgotten. The village of Krug, Happel, Michel ancestors that Grandpa spoke about became a dream to convert into reality. The only time Grandpa Henry Krug spoke in English was when he answered Enid's questions about the family German genealogy. Grandpa then talked about the family home in Löhlbach, Germany. He did not tell of its exact location because he only knew about it from talk with his immigrant father. It was inevitable that someday my family would travel to the village of our ancestors in Germany to research family genealogy. Grandpa Henry Krug spoke about the family home in the middle of Germany between two big rivers and how his parents moved to the middle of America between two big rivers, the Mississippi River and the Missouri River.

Acquaintance with a chaplain of our family's faith resulted in a conversation about the tour he was planning to Germany to attend the Oberammergau Passion Play 350th performance. When he learned of my heritage and interest in Germany he invited me to join him in organizing his tour. I became an escort and my airline ticket was arranged to travel to Germany in advance of the play to visit my ancestral villages. If I found and added enough travelers for his tour, my husband could also go free on the tour, and I had success in finding enough travelers for the tour so my husband could also go to Germany.

We flew to Amsterdam and rented a car to drive to Germany to the home of a German school teacher friend we had met when she visited her family in Oregon. It was not far from the Netherlands border to her home, and she accompanied us, reading the German language signs on the autobahn to Löhlbach. She interpreted the German language signs and interpreted all our speaking with German people since few in the villages speak English.

The pastor of the church in Löhlbach met us and invited us to the parsonage for dinner and to meet his family. We reciprocated by inviting the pastor and his family to the hotel dining room the following evening for dinner with us that was helpful in getting acquainted. We were in the village four nights and three days including a weekend so I could attend church on Sunday in the same building where my immigrant Krug ancestors were married December 25, 1835. It was called a "Homecoming Service" and I was given the opportunity to speak to the congregation. I was the first descendant of the six families who lived in the village and emmigrated to America in the 1850's and had never returned to the village.

My German vocabulary limited my speaking: "Ich danke Ihnen, Pastor Dressler. Ich frene mich sehr, hier in Löhlbach, in der Stadt meiner Vorfahren zu Sein und in Ihnen zu sprechen." (Translation: Thank you Pastor Dressler. I'm very happy to be here in Löhlbach in the city of my forefathers and to speak to you.) I then spoke in English and my accompanying German friend translated it into the German language for the congregation.

I enrolled in a German language course in college, but at that time it was not taught in the conversational method. The entire academic year German grammar was studied and the students' task was to translate Goethe writings.

Searching for the past of my family in Europe was not an easy task, especially as I am unaccustomed to their language and lacked knowledge of European history. I needed to gather information in a variety of ways that included personal interviews, research of church records, state archives, letters, newspapers and books, walks on the streets and paths of the villages—the gleaning of the story of an agrarian people of many centuries.

I could not speak German fluently or read the old style German language. The pastor of the Löhlbach church found a member in his congregation who was fluent in reading the old German records as well as speaking in German, and he was willing to work on my family research. He was allowed to take the history books from the church to a large room on the second floor of his home in the village where he searched and searched and found my ancestors. There were many books to search because each year had a separate book for births, confirmations, marriages, deaths that were listed in the order in which they occurred rather than in alphabetical order. It required lengthy years of research time.

To learn about my German heritage and gain a perspective of their immigration to the "new world" I visited the villages of Löhlbach, Haina, Sehlen, Altenhaina, Battenhausen, Dainrode, Sebbeterode, Grusen, Gemunden, Herbelhausen, Mohnhausen, and Dankerode-an-der-Fulda. The division by the Iron Curtain into East and West Germany was still in existence and the boundary was within thirty miles of my family villages.

I visited my ancestral homes, the home where my Great-Grandfather Krug was born in Löhlbach; the home where my Great-Great-Grandfather Happel was born in Altenhaina; the home of Great-Great Grandma Happel in Löhlbach; the home where Great-Great Grandma Krug was born in Löhlbach; and the home of my Werning ancestors in Dankerode-an-der-Fulda. The homes all still exist today much the same as in former years.

After this first visit to my heritage villages, I returned again nine more times and it was the ninth tine that I met my closest cousins, Krug 4th cousins who the church researcher found through the church records. In the records I learned the men in my family all were baptized Johann or Johannes which means, "God's Grace." I walked the streets of the village to find the house numbers listed in the church records where my relatives had been born and lived before emigration to USA. They all are still in existence.

In a drive to Altenhaina, called Alt Heim in earlier years, I saw the home of my Happel ancestors. The pastor drove us to Marburg, a university city with a population of 75,000 where state archives hold genealogical data and where the St. Elisabeth Cathedral holds the shrine of St. Elisabeth, the patron saint of Hessen, and the name sake of many of my German female relatives who were born both in Germany and America.

It was only a short distance to Dankerode-an-der-Fulda, not far from the East German border at that time, to the village of the Werning ancestors. The Werning home is right across the street from the Dankerode church where my ancestors were baptized, confirmed, and married. The home was still occupied by one of my relatives and he showed us the baptismal bowl and communion ware used by my ancestors that are still in use today in the church.

Engraved in stone along the door of the Dankerode church: Phil.1:21 Christus ist mein Leben, Und Sterben ist mein Gewinn. (For me to live is Christ, and to die is gain.) In the basement of the Werning home I saw the engraved stone in the foundation with the date 1833 and Werning name of my great-great-grandfather who built the house.

We drove to Wittenberg to see the Castle Church door where Luther posted the ninety-five theses that started the religious Reformation in centuries of the past.

Castle Church: (left to right)
Kenneth Palen, Richard Palen and Margaret Krug Palen

Luther's tomb (1483–1546) is below the pulpit in the Castle Church. We laid flowers on his tomb in memory of my German forefathers' religious life and heritage.

Martin Luther's tomb: (left to right)
Ken, Richard and Margaret Palen

Weimar, Germany, history begins in 975 A.D. and there we saw residences of many dukes. I viewed the statue of

Duke Karl August, 1757–1828, sitting on a horse that has one leg raised. Great-Uncle George Krug told me I would see "our Duke" when I talked with him about traveling to Löhlbach, the village of our Krug ancestors. He had learned about "our Duke" from his immigrant father and wished he could travel with me to Germany, but his ninety-plus years of age prevented him from going along with me at the time.

My second travel to Germany was only eight months after November 9, 1989 when the Berlin wall had fallen and the divided country was again one Germany. West Germany had risen economically like a phoenix from the ashes of World War II. My son Richard went with me and we picked up fragments of the Berlin wall and framed them upon returning home.

The civilization of the Romans is still in the shadows of Germany. The historical and artistic treasures of the people of Europe make it clear that the crown and the church possessed nearly all wealth and power in past centuries. The trickle of wealth and power to the middle class of Europe was slow. In my research I learned that people have very definite ideas about religion. They often look back to a golden age they think occurred in the early centuries after Christ's death when poverty and humility were preached, and every hardship shared lead to Heaven by morality and closeness to God.

In New York harbor I viewed "the golden door" and read the sonnet on the Statue of Libery: "Give me your tired, your poor, your huddled masses yearning to breathe free." It was my first conscious realization that the land of my birth recognized the feelings that welled up in me from my earliest memories of growing up in a European bilingual extended German Scottish farming family with aspirations and hope for attainments not previously known.

PART V

*Endurance produces character;
character produces hope...Romans 5:4*

CHAPTER 12
Understanding Cultures

In the three different years I traveled to Scotland I learned about my Scottish heritage and remembered what my great-grandmother said about the country.

"Welcome! Welcome! A thousand welcomes to God's country" the bus driver exclaimed when it was possible to see the huge boulder that sits high on the Cheviot Hills (1,371 feet) marking the entrance to Scotland.

Jedburg was the first stop in Scotland. The unicorn-topped column in the city square was the subject of cameras as was the Abbey and Mary Queen of Scot's nearby home containing her serene death mask of youthful features of forty-five years.

At a tour of Sir Walter Scott's country home I remembered reading "Lady of the Lake (1810) in high school English literature class.

Edinburgh Castle Esplanade was next and we had to be in our seats by 8:45 p.m. for the Tattoo—undoubtedly the finest spectacle of its kind in the world. Edinburgh Castle is on a rock of a dormant 20,000 year old volcano. St. Margaret's tiny chapel named after the Queen of Scotland AD 1047–1093; who built it was of interest to me.

The following days, I spent time at the General Register Office for Scotland, across the street from the Edinbugh Post Office, researching my highland and lowland family ancestors. A day permit to read the microfische of old handwritten brown ink records cost 4.50 pounds at that time. More time was needed to thoroughly search my ancestors. I continued work on it via mail.

England, an important heritage in my husband's family, was where he wanted first to travel and learn about his European heritage. It became so interesting to our family that our daughter elected to study at the University of London one term while she was a student at the University of Oregon. That was made possible through an exchange arrangement with professors of the two universities and her University of London credits earned counted toward her Oregon degree.

London is a friendly city, no language barrier, only idiomatic and metaphor differences. The imprint of the reign of Victoria and Albert on the city; England's heritage is indelibly found in the Royal Family. In this second Elizabethan age, the pomp and pageantry of royalty still stirs a patriotic interest in English genealogy.

Upon arrival in London we looked in a telephone directory of the city and discovered the listing of a Kenneth Palen name. The number was dialed and Kenneth Palen's mother answered. Kenneth Palen, a London fireman, was at work, but his mother was very interested in meeting us. She immediately came to our hotel. That was the beginning of a fascinating friendship. She had married her Kenneth Palen's father, a U.S. soldier on location in England. They divorced and she never remarried. Her son, named Kenneth, a London fireman, also came to meet us. We had dinner together and spent time getting acquainted. That was the beginning of a friendship that lasted the remainder of all our years. We visited them several times in England and they came to our Oregon home several years to visit us.

We looked forward to the changing of the guard at Buckingham Palace, the River Thames, St. Paul's Cathedral where my daughter and I took part in a communion service, Westminister Abbey where we saw the "stone of scone" and coronation chair, the Tower of London to see the "Star of India" diamond, crown jewels and coronation garments, Big Ben, Trafalgar Square, and Picadilly Circus.

We went to the theatre district on our London tour with our two teenagers and sat in the Phoenix Theatre dress circle to see *The Unvarnished Truth*, a humorous murder mystery. The second time we were in London we saw Andrew Lloyd

Webber's *Cats*. The third time we were in London we saw the longest running theatre play, Agatha Christie's *Mousetrap*.

We rode the black taxi cabs to the British Museum to see the finest collections in the world, a 200 year old treasure-house of international scholarship and picture-book of the history of man. There are so many artifacts from other civilizations that it made us aware of the British dominion over the world at a time when history was collectable.

We went to St. Catherine's House Government records to research my husband's family genealogy. His father always told him the Palens were originally from England and there was a county named Pale in early English history that was the beginning of the family name. The only records in St. Catherine's House are in handwriting since 1837, the first year of Queen Victoria's reign. The person helping with the research suggested we go to Ireland because there was a place in Ireland called "pale" and perhaps that was my husband's family origin.

Huntly Castle in Aberdeenshire is known as the "Cradle of the Gordons." I went there to see and experience the Gordon clan history.

In visits over the years to Great Britian, Scotland, and Ireland I observed remarkable change. Rollerbladers filled London's Trafagar Square instead of locals and tourists of earlier years. The number of travelers in those countries continued to increase in each year of my travels.

Cradle of the Gordon Clan
Huntly Castle, Scotland
Margaret Krug Palen is in the foreground

www.ingramcontent.com/pod-product-compliance
Lightning Source LLC
Chambersburg PA
CBHW050821160426
43192CB00010B/1850